WESTMINSTER PUBLIC LIBRARY

3 3020 01139 2734

UP AND AWAIR
BACK IN THE DAY

D0775362

MARY SCHAEFER

gatekeeper press

Columbus, Ohio

Westminster Public Library
3705 W. 112th Ave.
Westminster, CO 80031
DISCARD
www.westminsterlibrary.org

This book is a work of fiction. The names, characters and events in this book are the products of the author's imagination or are used fictitiously. Any similarity to real persons living or dead is coincidental and not intended by the author.

Up and Away – Back in the Day

Published by Gatekeeper Press
2167 Stringtown Rd, Suite 109
Columbus, OH 43123-2989
www.GatekeeperPress.com

Copyright © 2020 by Mary Schaefer
All rights reserved. Neither this book, nor any parts within it may be sold or reproduced in any form or by any electronic or mechanical means, including information storage and retrieval systems without permission in writing from the author. The only exception is by a reviewer, who may quote short excerpts in a review.

ISBN (paperback): 9781642377408
eISBN: 9781642377392

Library of Congress Control Number: 2020939331

To Mom, who saved all my letters
To Dad, who wondered why

Acknowledgments

One thousand thanks to Lisa Wroble, Rebecca Haun, Linda Platt, Judy Posser de Andrade, Jan Ellis, Dorothy Buddenhagen, Karen Bottemanne, Sarah Spencer, Madison Drake, and Joshua Kaplan for aiding and abetting. And, thanks also to the multitude of characters in the book who shared my adventures. I've changed your names, but you'll know who you are.

February 13, 1961

Dear Mother and Daddy –

I had an ominous feeling when my flight landed in Kansas City yesterday that something was about to go wrong. I was right. My flight arrived exactly on time. My suitcase arrived a couple of hours later. In San Francisco. Consequently, I had to report for my first day of training this morning without makeup (!), without clean underwear, and without that positive attitude and sunny disposition which is so prized by TWA, and for which, presumably, I have been hired.

Consider the irony: On my very first flight as a passenger on my new employer's airline, said airline loses my luggage.

After much wailing and gnashing of teeth on my part, I have been assured that my wayward suitcase has been captured, retagged and rerouted back to my loving arms and that I will have it tomorrow ... maybe. Meanwhile, I'm in what I believe is known in airline terms as a "holding pattern."

Must go now and write to Mary, my old roommate from college. She's back in her home town working at the job I've always shunned – the dreaded 9-to-5. After which, I plan to retire to my new bed. My kingdom for some pajamas! (Actually, it doesn't seem to be as important as it was back at the beginning of this letter.)

Love, Love, Love –
Christine

February 13, 1961

Hi, Mary —

This may turn out to be one of those yay/boo letters, because I'm going to tell you about yesterday, starting with my flight down to Kansas City for training. On boarding the plane, I was shown to a window seat in First Class (yay), and as I sat there congratulating myself on my good fortune, two toothpick-thin girls sat down behind me. Turns out they were also coming here for air hostess training. While I listened with my ears flapping, the two toothpicks began commiserating about how they both had to gain (!) weight to qualify for the job (boo). While, as you well know, I've been dieting for months — to the same end.

So, naturally, I was overjoyed (yay) when, after we landed and went to check into our motel apartments at the Skyline Inn, I was put in an apartment with three other girls who had already checked in, and those two toothpicks were put in the apartment next to me. Thus I was spared the agony of watching them tuck away the mashed potatoes and gravy for the next five weeks, while I subsist on carrot sticks and Metrecal (boo).

I really like two of my three roommates (yay). The one named Katy describes something she likes as "cool as a moose." And, the one named Suzanne was lamenting that, "My hair won't do what I want it to." So, Katy said, "What do you want it to do?" To which Suzanne replied, "Cook dinner."

Love,
Chris
P.S. My suitcase is lost (boo).

February 15, 1961

Dear Mother and Daddy –

If yesterday is any indication of the immediate future, we are not to be allowed a moment to spare. We began at oh six hundred (which is airline talk for 6:00 AM), and we didn't get to bed until 1:00 AM (oh one hundred). I suspect they are going to try to break us down with sleep deprivation. They bussed us to downtown Kansas City for our classes, where we got lectured to, welcomed several times, fingerprinted, weighed, measured, given books and makeup kits, taken on a tour of the building, and welcomed some more, all the while being made to feel like we were in a smiling contest. Somewhere along the way we were informed that TWA refers to us as "hostesses" rather than "stewardesses."

As promised, my errant suitcase made its way to my doorstep yesterday. I kissed it and forgave all, so it and I are a happy twosome again. I think my roommates are more relieved than I, as now I am all smiles and fairly fit to live with – in my moisturized, made-up face and clean underwear.

While we're not exactly wallowing in decadent luxury, our motel apartments are quite nice. There is a kitchen in each one, where we cook for ourselves – not one of my strengths. This morning I made my bed – now I'm going to lie in it.

Love, Love, Love –
Christine

February 15, 1961

Hi, Mary –

Both you and I know what a klutz I am in the kitchen, right? Well, we cook for ourselves here, so last night I bought a frozen chicken pot pie at the grocery store, and after we got home I stuck it in the oven, as per instructions. About a half hour later we smelled a weird burning odor coming from the kitchen, what the French might call *eau de plastique*. Well, you frankly have to wonder how I failed to grasp the fact that you are supposed to take the dumb thing out of the box first. But, how is the unsuspecting consumer supposed to know that? The directions made no mention of it at all.

One of my roommates commented helpfully, "If you had some bread, you could have a roast beef sandwich, if you had some roast beef."

Love – C
P.S. When we were at the grocery store, I also bought a 6-pack of Budweiser, which could have resulted in my being sent home immediately if I were caught. Well, my roommates were flabbergasted when they found out I did that, but be assured that they weren't too shocked to have one with me.

February 17, 1961

Dear Mom and Dad –

Today we had physicals. I passed. After that we went to the hangar and were shown all the parts, inside and out – of the Lockheed 049, which is one of the airplanes we will be working – and then we got to play with all the little gadgets in the galley (kitchen) and learned about all the emergency equipment. Then there was a lecture about speaking on the P.A. system, and we had our voices recorded. By the way, did you know that there is such a thing as a Midwest accent? Well, apparently there is, and I have one. (I heard myself on the P.A. saying "pyassengers.") Speaking of which, one of our instructors is from the South, and she told us today that we have the opportunity of a "lahf tom." (Susanne says she thinks there is corrective surgery for that accent.)

Later, while trying to remain respectfully alert, we were inflicted with an endless and less-than-riveting lecture on what makes airplanes fly and all about engines and blah blah blah. Then, after lunch, we perked up, because the speaker was a very virile looking captain, so when he started talking about "forward motion" and "upward thrust," we got all giggly.

Katy, my roommate, just went to bed, and as she was falling asleep, she said, "I can't wait to see the world – I've heard so much about it." Susanne says Katy is "anxious to be awed."

Love, Love, Love –
Christine

February 17, 1961

Hi, Mary –

Greetings from the Gulag! I've been here four days now, and it's really been a drag. We're so restricted that you'd think we were in a convent. There is no drinking during training – no dating on week nights – we can't leave the premises during the week except when we get bussed to downtown Kansas City to class, and we have to be in our apartments by 10:30 P.M. And, on weekends we can't go farther than 100 miles away. Woe betide us if we don't wear hose, heels and girdles at all times, hair no longer than chin length, and red lipstick and nail polish only. Very heavy going. ("Oh, where is the life that late I led?")

As I've mentioned, I have three roommates – I just love two of them. The other one is – dare I say it – a real snob. She's from New York and fancies herself veddy sophisticated. She doesn't acknowledge that there are any cities between New York and the West Coast - she calls everything in between "the third great ocean." Now, she is certainly entitled to her opinion, and far be it from me to suggest that she is a great big fathead.

So, I told her that last year I was Miss Illinois in the Miss America Beauty Pageant, that my dad is president of the World Bank and that my mother was an Olympic gold medal swimmer.

I didn't imagine she believed me, but it shut her up for a while. I think I could learn to like her – if she were suddenly to lapse into a deep coma.

Love –
Chris

February 18, 1961

Dear Mom and Dad –

We had the most fun today! We took what is known as a "Fright Flight." The whole class was taken up for a ride in the Convair 880 (jet). We flew up to 30,000 feet, and then we made an emergency nose dive at 1,600 feet a minute, just so we would know what it felt like. It felt exciting.

We had two tests this week – one on the emergency equipment on the Lockheed 049, plus one on Nomenclature, Terms and Definitions, Cabin management and Flight Procedures. I got a 96 and a 97, so I guess I'm safe for a while. Katy told us that a girl from her town went off to Kansas City with high hopes and a new hairdo, only to come slinking home a week later. Every now and then someone gets sent home – for what reason nobody seems to know, but rumors are flying. (Hey, did I just make a pun there?) Thus ends the first week of boot camp – four more to go before graduation. Gotta go study Flight Terminology, Uniform Requirements, Hostess Etiquette, Airline History, Company Personnel, Code Letters, Airplane Parts, etc. etc.

It's hard to concentrate on all this without having wild flights of fancy about the future. (Hey, was that another pun? I'm getting good at this.) We're being trained from the ground up. (I can't stop!) I just wanted to clear the air. (Okay, that's the last one.)

Love, Love, Love –
Christine
P.S. (I promise – this is the very last.) You're going to have a friend in high places.

February 19, 1961

Dear Mary –

Today was a very humbling day. In the morning we had a class given by a gorgeous red-haired model (who is absolutely free of brains, poor thing) about makeup and something called visual poise – translation: how to walk. In the afternoon we were escorted to Pierre's, which is apparently one of the most exclusive salons in Kansas City, to have our hair styled. (In my case, the hayseeds had to be removed first.) After being shampooed and curlered, and after sitting under the dryer for about a year, I was then combed, and teased into an exaggerated bouffant, ala Marie Antoinette. When I looked in the mirror, words failed me, and I'm told that, judging from the expression on my face, it was a good thing they did.

Tonight some of us are going to a party given by some students from a local dental college, no doubt resulting in a bit of reckless devilry. My roommate Katy cautions that we must be on guard against getting too giddy on mouthwash and laughing gas and missing the curfew time, thus getting fired and sent home, which would result in a tragic loss to the aviation industry.

Love,
Chris
P.S. In class the other day, we were being told how to greet passengers at the door of the aircraft by saying, "Good morning/afternoon/evening," and then perhaps a "jovial pleasantry," so my roommate Katy turned to me and said under her breath, "Good morning, sir. So a man and his monkey go into a bar......"

March 3, 1961

Dear Mother and Daddy –

Apparently by Monday we have to decide what city we want to be based in after graduation. (I know – it should be "in what city we want to be based.") Not that we will necessarily get our first choice, of course, but there are openings in Kansas City, New York, Chicago, and Los Angeles. Since I've never been out west, and since I guess it will be a bit on the chilly side everywhere else, I'm leaning ever so tentatively toward Los Angeles to begin my life anew. Meanwhile, the deadline looms.

Do you remember Jenny, one of my friends from college? She's been flying for United for about a year now and is transferring to Los Angeles next month, so she wants me to bid for L.A. and then we can get an apartment together at the beach. After which, in my preferred vision of the future, on our days off, we can resume our perpetual quest we started in college – to attain the perfect suntan.

Actually, I just found out today, to my considerable surprise, that when we first start flying we'll be on Reserve for at least a couple of months, which means I will be sitting at home "on call," waiting to fly – who knows where – on any type of airplane – at any time. Should be fun. Or could be awful. You can be sure I will let you know which.

Love, Love, Love –
Christine

March 3, 1961

Hi, Mary –

Oh woe! I've been suffering under the delusion that I would soon be winging my way to the farthest corners of the world, but, *au contraire!* I just found out today that new-hires are not eligible to fly International flights until we've been flying Domestic for TWO YEARS!! BUGGER! Meanwhile, wherever I'm based in these United States you must catapult yourself thereto – with utmost dispatch. I'm hoping it will be Los Angeles, so if you have a couple of fingers you're not using, please cross them for me.

My snot roommate continues to annoy – with her quasi-sophistication. Another reason to be based in Los Angeles – to get as far away from her as possible. She, of course, would consider suicide (not a bad idea) if she were based anywhere but her precious New York. She said to me today, "Doubtless you will go to Los Angeles." "Doubtless," I said.

Love,
Chris
P.S. Crack out that quill pen and parchment paper and write me soon and often.

March 16, 1961

Hi, Mom and Dad –

News Bulletin! Tomorrow morning at 08:30 we graduate! And receive our wings! (Which is actually a pin with only one wing – the pilots get a pin with the full set of two.)

This morning we had our final exam, which covered the 049, 749, Super G, Convair 880 and Boeing 707 airplanes. Then, after passing said exam and after promising to love, honor, and obey TWA, our leg irons were struck off, and we were given the rest of the day to pack and get ready to go out into the world and make good. And – guess what – I'm going to be making good in Los Angeles! That is, if one can make good on a whopping $300 a month, which is to be our salary beginning Monday. So, it would appear likely that my primary method of communicating with you will be a continuation of periodic letters, rather than the more costly alternative of calling on the telephone. Can one subsist on $300 a month, you might well ask? I fervently hope so.

There are nine of us poised to depart to LAX (airline code letters for Los Angeles). Katy refers to us as "the huddled masses yearning to breathe smog."

Love, Love, Love –
Christine

March 16, 1961

Guess what, Mary – tomorrow I begin my new life – in the City of Our Lady the Queen of Angels – better known as Los Angeles! And guess who my roommates will be – the two toothpicks I told you about! Turns out they're both really nice – they've asked me to get an apartment with them in Santa Monica – at least until Jenny hits town – then the two of us will move down to Manhattan Beach, which is really close to the airport.

So, our plan is to graduate tomorrow morning and then have a class picture taken, outfitted in our new TWA finery – then catch the 12:30 flight to L.A. – find an apartment on Sunday, and – assuming the gods are smiling on us – be ensconced in same by Monday, at which time we will report for our orientation meeting at the hangar. Can we do it? You betcha.

Susanne and Katy are going to be based in New York – along with most of the class – so we're making elaborate plans to see each other – when I have layovers in New York and when they have layovers in L.A. You will love them – they are such dears! Susanne is a cute, petite brunette, and Katy is a really pretty strawberry blond.

Gotta fold in my limbs and hit the sack now – I must be upright at dawn. Romance and adventure beckon!

Love,
Chris

March 21, 1961

Dear Folks –

Today was the longest day of my life.

I just got into my hotel room here in Kansas City (safe from all the "slings and arrows of outrageous fortune") after working my first flight. Here's how it went:

I had to get up at 3:45 A.M. in Los Angeles (not an hour with which I have much familiarity).

I was working with two other girls who are best friends, so they talked only to each other.

The plane was packed to the gills all three legs.

We served breakfast from LAX to Phoenix.

We served coffee from Phoenix to Albuquerque.

We served lunch from Albuquerque to Kansas City.

Apparently we flew over Superstition Mountain and the Painted Desert, but I was too busy lurching up and down the aisle, trying to keep my balance, to even glance out the window. When I first ventured into that mysterious region beyond the cockpit door, the pilots were looking out the window, so I had to talk into the backs of their heads. But, when they learned it was my first flight, they were nice enough to invite me to sit with them in the cockpit for takeoffs and landings and to let me wear headphones so I could listen to them talking to the control tower.

It's beyond my capacity to guess what fresh horrors are in store for me tomorrow. All I know is that I go back to LAX on an 049, which is a small prop plane, so the good news is that we have only a beverage service on each leg, but the bad news is that it takes 9 ½ hours to get there. (Gives new meaning to the term "non-stop flight," huh?)

Then I have one day off, a class the next day, and then on Reserve for several months.

I feel like I've put in as arduous a day as any mortal ever did, so now I'm going to go dissolve into my bed and try to catch up on about six weeks of sleep.

Love, Love, Love –
Christine

March 21, 1961

Hi, Mary–

As it turns out, I was so eager to rush out and seize the world by the throat that I neglected to consider that being a hostess might entail some real effort. I'm on my first layover – in my first hotel room, and I feel like something that was washed up by the tide. The flight here was pretty rough – not weather wise, but it had a distinct resemblance to actual hard work. We were bustling around like rats in a maze, with no time even to look down at the fruited plain we were flying over. Of course, I have nothing to compare it to, but I can only hope all my flights won't be like today's. I feel pretty sure it's not something I'll look back on with nostalgia.

Our apartment in Santa Monica is really cute – pink stucco, built around a courtyard with palms and ferns. We're on the second floor – one bedroom with three beds, and it costs us each $46.67 a month, plus utilities. And we didn't have to sign a lease! When we go to the airport, we can just walk over a few blocks to the Miramar Hotel and take the shuttle.

My toothpick roommates both chose LAX as their base in order to be closer to their boyfriends – JoBeth's lives in San Francisco and is a stockbroker, and LeeAnn's lives in Hollywood and is trying to break into the movies. More about them later.

Meanwhile, we are looking forward to that first paycheck like it was the second coming.

Love,
Chris

March 26, 1961

Dear Folks –

Have you been sitting around day after day longing for that dream vacation for two? How about the sunny shores of Miami? Games of luck in Las Vegas? The Hollywood Hills? The cable cars of San Francisco? London theatre? Paris cafes? Well, your dreams have just come true. Or, at least they will in six months, at which time I get off probation and become eligible for four free passes on TWA for me and/ or my parents, to be used - within a year - anywhere TWA flies. They are standby passes, so if you don't try to travel in the summer months or on the week end, you shouldn't have any problem getting seats. Unless I've been grossly mislead.

Tomorrow I'm working a flight to New York – my first on a jet. It's a check ride, which means that my supervisor goes along to check me out. I'm pretty nervous about it, but my roommate just said to me, "It's a long flight – you're bound to do something right." My other roommate quoted Spencer Tracy's advice to novice actors: "Just know your lines and don't bump into the furniture." Since it's my first trip to New York, I'm burning up the brain cells trying to figure out how to see the whole city on a one-day layover. I'm all aquiver with anticipation.

Guess I'd better go study the Convair 880 and the Boeing 707, so I'll look like I know what I'm doing on the morrow when I'm released on the unsuspecting passengers

Love, Love, Love
Christine

March 26, 1961

Hi, Mary –

Today my roommates and I finally got a chance to stroll down to the beach and stick our toes in the Pacific Ocean. Remember when we used to go to Ft. Lauderdale on spring break? Well, it felt just like the Atlantic – except that the water is a LOT colder! The rest of my bod is going to have to wait until the weather warms up – perhaps in August – for that full-body plunge it was so looking forward to.

Last night we met my roommate LeeAnn's boyfriend. His name is Lee, also. Lee Something-Or-Other. So, if (God forbid) they ever got married, they would have the same names. She clings to him like she's been grafted on. He's kind of cute, but I fear he has only the very minimum number of brain cells. In a moment of weakness (actually, after ingesting a few gin-and-tonics) LeeAnn confessed to us the other night that her Lee has a foot fetish. Seems that when he was little, his mother was a hair dresser, and she would take him to work with her every day, so he would sit on the floor and look at the ladies' feet all the time. Now, when he and LeeAnn get together, they go to his apartment, and he paints her toenails over and over, and that's it. That's all they do. At least she says that's all they do.

After consulting my book of clichés, the best I can come up with is, "To each his own."

Love,
Chris

March 27, 1961

Dear Mother and Daddy –

Today I got through my first jet flight (that is, the outbound half of the trip) relatively unscathed. I was B hostess, which meant that I worked in the galley in first class and predictably burned my fingers numerous times. We had a ground stop in Las Vegas and were supposed to have another stop at O'Hare before coming here to New York, but there were bodacious winds around Chicago, so we had to land in Dayton, Ohio instead, which didn't go over at all well with the inmates. (In fact, one of the passengers pulled out a map and asked me to take it up to the cockpit.) The angry hordes that were bound for Chicago were acting peevish, so we gave everyone free drinks. I thought that was a capital idea, so I suggested to my supervisor that TWA should always give free drinks on every flight – even to the crew. (I was counting on her good sense of humor.) At the end of the flight, she assured me that I did "a good job." So, who am I to disagree?

Tomorrow we go back to L.A. at 4:30 P.M. (or in airline lingo, 16:30 – everything is done on the 24-hour clock). I'm going to be "A" hostess, so I get to make the announcements (not one of my strengths) and open and close the door and pour champagne (is one of my strengths). Considering my supervisor will be monitoring my every move, I'm not facing tomorrow with overweening enthusiasm.

Love, Love, Love –
Christine

March 28, 1961

Hi, Mary –

Just got back from New York City! It was my first trip there, and I had made very ambitious sightseeing plans, but it turned out that my flying partner and I slept until 10:30 on the day of our layover, which meant that we had only a few hours to see the city. We took the elevator to the top of the Empire State Building and looked down (so, technically we did see the whole city) and then took a subway to Washington Square and walked around observing dove droppings and dog doo.

This trip was my first time working a jet, and it was a check ride, which means that my supervisor went along to make sure I was on my toes, so I was pretty nervous. On the return trip home yesterday I was working "A" hostess on a Boeing 707, which holds 16 first class passengers, to which we were to serve a five-course dinner with all the frills, and I was in charge! After takeoff I proceeded to set up the serving cart just the way we were taught in training, with 16 napkins, 16 forks, 16 spoons, 16 knives, 16 wine glasses, 16 water glasses, and 16 salt and pepper shakers. After which I turned proudly to my supervisor, hoping for a sign of approval from her, but instead she said to me, "That looks lovely, Chris, but did you really need to go to all that trouble for just one passenger?" Seems I was so engrossed in the elaborate ritual of setting up the cart that I failed to look back into the first class cabin, which – sure enough – contained one solitary man.

Love,
Chris

April 3, 1961

Dear Folks –

In the Good News Department, I'm flying with my roommate JoBeth this month. Our layovers are in Albuquerque, which is not exactly Fun Fest USA, but we stay at a nice hotel with a big pool – all the better to work on acquiring that perfect suntan. The captain says we treat sunbathing with all the diligence of an Olympic event.

Our first flight was on April 1, so all that day I made sure to maintain a super alert attitude, lest someone play some moronic joke on me. I successfully fended off a few lame efforts (no less than five people told me my slip was showing – it wasn't) and thus got through the day with no major embarrassments. I did pull a good one on the captain, though. I told him he had a booger hanging out of his nose. He wasn't amused. In fact, he told me to go somewhere and finish evolving.

On the flight over we had Richard Boone and the whole crew from *Have Gun, Will Travel* on board - they were really a rowdy bunch, and a lot of fun. George Hamilton was also on the flight, but he was very quiet – just sat there and looked gorgeous.

Today we were supposed to go to the Don Loper studio in downtown L.A. to get fitted for our new summer uniforms, but my roommates won't get out of bed. Any hope of rousing them is remote at best. So, I guess I'll take myself to the beach instead.

Love, Love, Love –
Christine

April 3, 1961

Hi, Mary –

I now know from firsthand experience the meaning of the term "irate passenger."

Yesterday I worked a trip home from Albuquerque with my roommate JoBeth. I was working the galley, setting up the meal trays and whipping out the hot entrees from oven to meal tray, and JoBeth was serving the trays to the passengers. After she placed a tray in front of a very dignified man, he asked her for a pillow, so when she opened the overhead rack to get him one, his hat fell out of the rack and landed upside down right into his Lobster Thermidor!

Well, first his nostrils flared, then his face got all red and contorted, and then he let out a howl of anguish. He was so angry, he got his words all mixed up and called her a "lung yady" and said he was going to have her job. The obvious answer would have been, "You can have it, but you wouldn't like it," but she bit her tongue. He was so mad I thought he was actually foaming at the mouth, but JoBeth said it was just some unswallowed mashed potatoes.

Evidently he must have really liked that hat. It was nice – a pale grey Homberg with a pale grey ribbon. A nice contrast to his crimson face.

As for JoBeth, she looked as if she would very much have liked to be elsewhere. I was so proud of her for being able to placate him the way she did. I'm sure I couldn't placate my way out of a paper bag.

I'm at the beach right now, and I've just experienced a structural failure (the zipper on my bathing suit broke), so I guess I'd better hightail it home.

Love,
Chris

April 20, 1961

Dear Ones –

Good times abound! Mary, my old roommate from college, flew out here last week to spend my 5-day spread with me. In case I haven't explained this before, when we're on Reserve, we get a period of five consecutive days during each month when we're free of all duty– and my spread was last week.

On Monday we went shopping in Beverly Hills – the kind of shopping that is a multi-sensory experience of looking, touching, smelling – occasionally trying on – but not buying. I'll be deferring that pleasure until I get on my feet financially – like maybe sometime in 1984. That night we walked over to the Santa Monica Civic Auditorium and ogled movie stars going into the Academy Awards, the high point of which was seeing Elizabeth Taylor in a white fur coat, wowing the cheering horde of onlookers.

One day we rented a car and drove down to Disneyland, only to find it closed that day, so we drove over to CBS to see a TV show being filmed, but there weren't any good ones on that day. Check and checkmate.

So that the day wouldn't be a total loss, we drove around to see some of the places we'd heard of – Dino's (Dean Martin's bar), the Crazy Horse (used to be Ciro's), Albatross, Red Banjo, etc. After which we drove down to POP, which is an amusement park on a cliff overlooking the ocean, and rode the carrousel with mad abandon.

You'll be so proud of me – one morning I cooked scrambled eggs and toast for Mary and me! We had to throw away the burned bacon, but after a slight scraping off of the toast, it was actually quite edible. Mary did wonder, though, how I could get the bacon so black without burning down the building.

Mary is TOO much fun – JoBeth told her that TWA stands for "Travel with Angels." So, Mary said no, she heard it stood for "Try Walking Across." She thinks we should name our apartment. You know, like the way rich people name their estates? JoBeth suggested Pink Palace. LeeAnn preferred Major Manor, both of which failed to generate much enthusiasm. But, Mary's idea prevailed – we've named it Upsand Downs.

When she left to go home and was hugging my two toothpick roommates, she ventured to say that she could put her arms around both of them at once – and still have room for a couple more people.

Love, Love, Love –
Christine

April 28, 1961 –

Dear Folks –

I've only been a hostess for about three minutes, and already I've had a modicum of excitement – it came on my last flight, in the form of an emergency – of sorts. Here's what happened: We were on a Convair 880, about ¾ of the way home from Chicago, when all of a sudden the oxygen masks fell down from overhead. We were all just sort of puzzled until the captain came on the P.A. and announced that the airplane had lost cabin pressure and that we were descending to 7,000 feet and would remain at that altitude for the rest of the flight. That's all there was to it, really. Nobody ever actually put on a mask – we just sort of ignored them – like it wasn't happening. I'm so new at this job that I didn't know enough to be concerned, which in retrospect was a good thing because the passengers look to us to see how we are reacting. And, since we were sort of ho-hum about it, no one ever panicked.

Later, on the crew bus we were talking about how the masks fell down, and the captain said, "Oh, did the masks fall down?" Seems like he should have known that, but, on second thought, how would he?

Oh, and on a recent flight to Las Vegas we had Joe Louis on board! I know what a fight fan you are, Daddy, so I thought about you and wished you had been there. What a nice man he is! I was surprised to notice that he had smaller-than-average hands.

Gotta flee –
Love, Love, Love –
Christine

24

April 28, 1961

Hi, Mary –

What a fun flight I had last week! I was flying with my roommate JoBeth, and guess who we had on flight – Victor Borge! He is absolutely THE most hilarious man alive! He kept up a running monologue of witty remarks through the whole flight. I was sitting across from him on takeoff, and he said to me, "Fasten your girdle, little girl." We kept hovering around him every chance we got, so we wouldn't miss anything he said. When we were serving meals, he told the lady across from him to, "Keep your bib clean." And when I asked him if I could serve him lunch, he said, "I'd be devastated if you didn't." As he was deplaning, he said to me, "It was a delightful flight. They'll never be able to take that away from us."

It was after our next flight that we were called in to the Gestapo, in the form of our supervisor, for a grooming check. It began mitt der patting of der hienies to make sure we were wearing our girdles. Then, I was told that I had been seen not wearing my hideous, detestable hat (my adjectives, not hers). The company rule is, "Wheels up, hats off – wheels down, hats on." So, when I'm on a flight with a couple of whistle stops, I don't bother putting it on each time. I hate the blasted thing anyway – it looks like a mushroom with a pancake on top. Apparently, she didn't want my head on a platter – she just wanted a hat on it.

So, I was duly chastised for that, and then she instructed JoBeth in her authoritative way, that her cuticles needed pushing back - and we were let go mitt ein warning.

Lordy, Lordy –
Chris

May 17, 1961

Dear Mom and Dad —

This is shaping up to be an excellent month! Reserve has been pretty slow — actually I haven't worked for about ten days. Jenny's transfer came through — she's been here for a couple of weeks, so we were able to go apartment hunting in Manhattan Beach, and the first day we found one that we just LOVE and were able to move into it right away.

Our groovy new abode is only one block from the beach — upstairs over a garage. It has a kitchen, a bedroom and a living room with a fireplace that has picture windows on either side, so we can watch the gorgeous sunsets over the ocean. And my part of the rent is only $10 a month more than I have been paying! Yay!

We've already thrown our first party — with a few guys we met at the beach. We were celebrating the fact that one of them had broken the habit of a lifetime and gotten a job. As we were toasting him, he said, "I love the taste of booze. It's one of the big advantages of being an alcoholic."

There are four of them who live together. Three of them are from back east, and their accents are a gas — they sound like gangsters right out of a B movie. One of them has an accent that falls in a sub-category of its own. The other day he was waxing on about how much he loves the weather here in California, and he said, "Da wind hits yuhs in da face..." And, the other night he said, "Wadda we gonna do at ten toidy on a Toisday night?"

Jenny calls it "cross-cultural communication."

Love, Love, Love —
Christine

May 17, 1961

Hi, Mary –

It's official! I'm a beach bum! Jenny's here – we found an apartment at the beach – moved right in – made contact with fellow beach bums. The gods are smiling on us.

We gave our first party for a guy who just got a job – something with which he has little familiarity. As we toasted him, he announced, "Some guys work their whole lives with nothing to show for it. I already have that."

I think Jenny and I are going to make ideal roommates. She says her idea of housework is to sweep the room with a glance. For my part, the last time I dusted anything, dinosaurs were still wandering around on the earth.

Not unlike many other airline apartments around the country, I suspect, a number of our kitchen utensils are courtesy of TWA. Jenny says I must stop taking the silverware from the airplane, or the company is going to have a bad year. I've noticed, however, that she occasionally reroutes the odd bottle of wine.

We've named our new abode Sandy Manor. For obvious reasons.

Bye for now – Chris
P.S. Do you know how you can tell an Alitalia airplane? It has hair under its wings.

June 12, 1961

Dear Mom and Dad –

I've had the best run of luck lately – I had a trip to Las Vegas last week, which was scheduled for a one-day layover, but after we got there our return flight cancelled, so our layover turned out to be three days long. We stayed at the Sands hotel, and the first night we went to Frank Sinatra's show. And then we saw him again the next day walking around the pool. Far out!

The next night we went to Milton Berle's opening night at the Flamingo. As you might expect, Uncle Miltie is a lot more raw in his live act than he is on TV.

The next day we got a bunch of coins and played the slot machines, and guess what! I won $25! But then, as you might have guessed, I lost $15 of it on another machine.

In a fit of madness I broke down and bought a two-piece bathing suit while I was there. Seems they are all the rage this year. It feels so odd to have my stomach showing – like those dreams you have where you are walking around someplace where there lots of people, and all of a sudden you realize, much to your chagrin, that you are the only one who is naked.

I went to a barbeque the other night at a house on the beach in Santa Monica next to Peter Lawford's place. We kept peeking over at his house to get a glimpse of him, but no luck there.

Love, Love, Love –
Christine

June 12, 1961

Mary –

Wherefore art thou? Haven't heard from you for a while.

Oh, Mary - you absolutely must move out here – the dating scene is a blast! In the last few weeks I've been out with a TV writer, a doctor of endocrine glands who is from Chile, a salesman for Kaiser Aluminum, a guy who designs greeting cards, a 6'4" redheaded ex-Marine, a soon-to-be child psychologist, a typewriter salesman, and a pilot from one of my flights. So, come on out and get in on the fun!

Harry Belafonte is performing in town this week, and I've had two offers to go see him, so I should get there at least once, if I don't have to fly.

Actually, I do have to work occasionally – to ensure me the three squares a day. After which I'm able to proceed to the more important matter – of dating.

Have you read the book *Hawaii*? I'm about half-way through it, and I really love it. Get out here – now!

Love, Chris
P.S. I bought a two-piece bathing suit – it just screams, "Ogle me!"

July 30, 1961

Dear Mother and Daddy –

Guess what! We have a new roommate! She's a sweet little thing with grey hair and sort of big ears. Her name is Felina, and she licked me awake this morning. Don't panic! She's a lovely little kitten. She has a very intelligent looking face, so this morning when she jumped up on the kitchen table in front of me and sat looking at me, exposing her soft, white underbelly, I decided to take advantage of the opportunity to try to fathom the inner workings of the feline mind. I looked deep into her eyes and asked her if she is happy living here with us at Sandy Manor. She blinked, stared at me for a while, then looked off into space, closed her eyes and yawned, then jumped down to the floor and ambled away. I took that as a "yes."

To answer your question about our layovers, mom – yes, the company does reserve hotel rooms for us, and they are paid for by the airline. There is always a limo or van waiting to drive us to the hotel after our flight arrives. We pay for our own meals while on layovers, but we get a per diem allowance which, along with our overtime pay, we receive, in the form of an expense check on the 15th of the following month. Overtime is considered as any hours flown over 73 hours a month. Since my basic pay is a paltry $308 a month after taxes, that expense check is welcomed like manna from heaven.

Your "poor" dear daughter –
Christine

July 30, 1961

Hi, Mary –

Have I told you about Burt? He's front and center right now – in fact, I guess you could say he's my new boyfriend. He's an artist, but he also works at the local liquor shop. He's not what you might call handsome, but the fact that he likes to DO things, rather than just sitting around talking about them is a very attractive quality. And, he does seem to know how to do lots of things.

We always play chess or gin rummy at the beach – and he's taken me water skiing and horseback riding. (I asked him, "Do you like horses?" and he answered, "I've met so few.") Yesterday we hung a "Gone Fishing" sign on the door and actually went fishing.

The other night he showed me how to make shrimp and French fries. And, tonight we were going to make barbeque sandwiches. Unfortunately, last night he got mad at me and walked out, so maybe I won't be seeing him again. Oh well … he is many wonderful things, but wealthy isn't one of them. He may have even less $ than I do. Which is none. At all.

Love,
Chris
P.S. We've adopted a cat – I'm hoping to train her to pick me up at the airport.

September 6, 1961

Dear Mother and Daddy –

Hooray! Time to whip out the champagne and celebrate! Your No. 2 daughter is now a full-fledged bone fide TWA hostess in good standing. We've made it through our six-month Review of Emergency Procedures, which was a prerequisite to being officially declared off probation. (Applause here.)

So, unless we are visited by some world-shaking cataclysmic event, such as another ice age, or an infestation of deadly organisms, or an invasion of aliens from Pluto (the planet – not the Disney character), it would appear I will be keeping this cushy job for a while longer.

Now for my least favorite topic of chat. I'm well aware of what a world-class, natural-born worrier you are, mom. And, human nature being what it is, I realize that it's impossible for one to stop worrying about something just because one is told to. Nevertheless, I'm asking you to do just that. Stop worrying about me. We've been told that only one flight of every 38,000 crashes. Pretty good odds, huh?

And now, dear readers, please excuse me while I go slip into something comfortable – like a nourishing gin and tonic.

Much Love,
Christine

September 6, 1961

Hi, Mary –

Now for the second and final chapter of the Burt story. In the last chapter, you may remember, he got mad and stomped out. When he made his reentry a few days later, I realized that I hadn't missed him at all. In fact, it gave me a chance to reflect on what the ultimate outcome would be if we became serious. I was in danger of being stuck living in Manhattan Beach for the rest of my life! I would never get to Europe! Or Asia! Or anywhere! So consequently, we're no longer in each other's orbit. Close call, huh?

But, tomorrow night I have a blind date with Bob Somebody, who graduated from Harvard and used to be a bouncer in Bermuda, so that ought to prove … at the least … interesting.

Last week Jenny and I and the four guys from the beach that we hang out with drove down to Tijuana for the day. We rode on a donkey (the sign advertised, "Ride on Your Own Ass!"), went to the Bullfights at the Toreo de Tijuana, and then ate tacos and drank lots and lots and lots of tequila – after which I almost got married to one of them. I don't even remember which one. Close call, huh?

Love,
Chris
P.S. Jenny had a guy on one of her flights who told her that his wife didn't understand him – she speaks Portuguese.

October 1, 1961

Hi, Folks –

I've just given birth. To an idea. (Had you there for a second, didn't I?) As I may have mentioned before, my roommate JoBeth's boyfriend lives in San Francisco, so she's planning to transfer there as soon as there are openings. (I suspect her underlying motive is to audition for the roll of Mrs. Boyfriend.) Anyhow, I'm thinking this may be just the opportune time – while the spirit moves me - to do the same, in order to get away from the beach crowd and move on toward new horizons. Neither of us can afford to move just yet – Jenny says the problem is that we have too much month left at the end of our money.

So, as a result, we're in that deep gulf between conception and realization. (Isn't that a nifty phrase? I read it somewhere.)

Had you been gazing out the window a few hours ago, you would have seen me flying over you – on my way home from Boston. It was the first time there for me – and actually for the whole crew. We had a great layover – we took a city tour – saw lots of famous historical stuff.

Love, Love, Love –
Christine
P.S. I learned something new on that flight. The Passenger Call Button is used to indicate to the hostess that you do not realize that your call button is on.

October 1, 1961

Dear Mary –

Just got back from the best trip – to Boston. It was the first time there for the whole crew, so we really knocked ourselves out to see everything in one day. We took a bus tour of the city—went into Paul Revere's house, saw the Old North Church and also Old Ironsides (U.S.S. Constitution). And a bunch of other stuff.

I have three more trips there this month, but I'm going to try to trade them for Pittsburgh trips as often as I can. Whatever for? you may be wondering. Here's why: My last trip there I met The Man!!! His name is Hank, he's 24 and is an architect (studied under Frank Lloyd Wright) and is in business with another guy. His only egregious fault is that, instead of looking you in the eye, he sort of looks you in the nose, which gives him the appearance of being slightly cross eyed.

He has bundles of $, and I just love him!

Romance beckons!

Later – Chris
P.S. Do you know how you can tell a motorcycle rider is happy? He has bugs on his teeth.

November 2, 1961

Dear Parents –

May I venture to remind you that in February, a scant three months away, I will be getting four free passes on TWA – good until the following February - to be used anytime, anywhere that TWA flies – by me or my parents, who just happen to be you two? So, dear readers, at last your investment in No. 2 daughter will begin to pay off.

I can see it now – the two of you sitting at a sidewalk café in Paris, lifting your aperitifs in a toast to TWA and to each other for surviving all the tribulations of raising a dimwit daughter. Anyway, let me know by and by when and where you want to go, and I'll put in for the passes. Preferably soon – before I get fired for not wearing my hat. Or for some other inane reason.

In re: Thanksgiving – Jenny and her boyfriend and I and two other girls plus the four guys that we hang out with (we call them Our Gang) are going to cook a turkey dinner in our kitchen. The only problem being that none of us knows how. Do you have any pointers for us, mom?

How do you make that wonderful cranberry salad you always make? And, how do you make cloverleaf rolls? And, how do you make dressing? And, how do you make a turkey?

Love, Love, Love –
Christine
P.S. Jenny's boyfriend advises us on our foray into the kitchen, "First – do no harm."

November 2, 1961

Hi, Mary –

Well, I'm not going to see Hank ever again. I've decided he's a creep, and I've removed my tentacles from him. We made a perfect couple – except for him. It's just as well, because I'm flying to Dayton this month, and it's very difficult to trade out of those trips. For obvious reasons.

Just found out that my vacation is the first half of February, so do you wanna do something fun? Maybe something that doesn't cost a whole lot of money? Also, I may be transferring to San Francisco at some point, so I want you to visit me there, if you can swing it. There are lots of places to go there to hear jazz and lots of sightseeing stuff to do.

We are moving into our beautiful new airport here in L.A. today. United was the first to move into their terminal, and I believe American will be in theirs soon. It will be a mess for a while, as nobody knows where to go – and our building isn't even finished yet.

Jenny is in Baltimore today, so I'm having a lazy day in residence here in Sandy Manor – reading and writing letters and entertaining deep thoughts. Just finished **Nine Stories** by J.D. Salinger – have you read it? Do. I'm just starting **Madame Bovary** – it's brilliant.

Love,
Chris

December 1, 1961

Dear Mother and Daddy –

Bugger! Bugger! Bugger! The sad fact is that I won't be able to make it home for Christmas. Our trip with the 3-day layover in Chicago will no longer operate after December 14. As it stands, like it or not (NOT!), I will be in St. Louis for Christmas and in Philadelphia on New Year's Eve. No getting around it, I guess. But, on the bright side, my vacation is the first half of February, so maybe I can spend a few days of it with you. OR, better yet, you could use your passes to come to the west coast to see me. Or, we could go somewhere together. Ponder that.

Our Thanksgiving turkey dinner was less than a resounding success. But, for someone who heretofore couldn't even fry water, I think I've come a long way. Or, maybe just a short way. Anyhow, we had lots (and lots) of champagne, so we all had a blissful day. Correct me if I'm wrong, but I think it was Churchill who said, "Success is going from failure to failure with enthusiasm."

In the Good News Department – Jenny is going to marry her boyfriend sometime soon. That will work out well, as JoBeth and I have put in for our transfers to San Francisco.

Adventure Beckons!

Love, Love, Love – Christine
P.S. Have you read **Breakfast at Tiffany's**? Do. It's a good read.

December 1, 1961

Hi, Mary —

It's official! Our little Jenny is getting married! Oh woe! It is going to be such a colossal loss to the male population of the Western world.

Our Thanksgiving turkey dinner may well come under the heading of – fiasco. I ended up doing most of the cooking, because we had it at our apartment (hereinafter known as "the scene of the crime"). First of all, I was led to believe the turkey would take 2 ½ hours to bake. It actually took 7. The cranberry Jello salad didn't set, so it was all runny. Jenny's boyfriend said it "lacked definition." The cloverleaf rolls were rock hard. In fact one of the guys told me to save them, and tomorrow we would take them to the driving range. And someone else said, "The rolls weren't bad, but maybe you should have used flour instead of cement." Also, I burned the graham cracker crust on the pumpkin pie, and the inside was sort of like pudding. So, it, too, "lacked definition."

Nevertheless, I plan to soldier on in my relentless quest for – let's just say "adequacy" in the kitchen.

Love, Chris
P.S. String some sentences together and send them to me.

December 20, 1961

Dear Folks –

Thanx 1,000,000 (thank you, thank you, thank you, etc.) for all the nice things you sent me for Christmas. I love everything. The pillow you made is really beautiful, Mom, and VERY clever. Was that your idea to weave all those ribbons in and out? It will go perfectly in the chic new apartment that JoBeth and I are planning to get in SFO (San Francisco).

I was shocked to the core of my being to learn that Mary is getting married! – sometime between Christmas and New Year's. What a total surprise! Apparently, she's marrying a guy who works in her office. I've never met him. Or even heard of him. I fervently hope he is sufficiently deserving of her. There seems to be a number of troth plighters in my life lately, huh?

I'm finding myself in the unenviable position of having to arise from my bed at 5:30 AM on Christmas morning and spend the bulk of the day on the airplane. However, I will be just one of a planeload full of people, all wishing we were somewhere else. On the plus side, there probably won't be too many of what Jenny calls the "slavering hordes" traveling that day.

Have a lovely Christmas – I bid you be merry and of good cheer.

Love, Love, Love,
Christine

December 20, 1961

Oh, Mary –

Oh! Oh! Oh! (That sound you just heard is my jaw hitting the floor.) I am exceedingly shocked and excited to hear that you will soon be in a state of holy matrimony! *Tres jolie!* I'm pleased beyond all proportion! The happy news sent the blood coursing joyously through my veins.

What is his name? What does he look like? Fair or dark? Young or old? Tall or small? How long have you been seeing each other? (Every day at work, obviously, but you know what I mean.) What kind of wedding will you have? Where will you honeymoon? Enlighten me. Sounds like your holiday season will be a nonstop celebration.

My life, on the other hand, is not quite as *jolie.* Picture this: its 9 PM, and I'm here in Sandy Manor getting ready to go out on flight, i.e. applying my mask, donning the uniform, combing the crowning glory, etc. The phone rings. "Hello," says I. "Is this Christine?" says a female voice. "Yes," says I, predictably. "This is your supervisor – did you know that you had a flight tonight?" says she. "Yes, it leaves at 11:00 – I'll be there," says I, reassuringly. Pause. "It left at 9:00 – without you!" bellowed she.

Apparently, I got the numbers of the 24-hour clock mixed up and made the perfectly natural mistake of thinking 2100 was 11 o'clock. Well, my supervisor didn't think it was perfectly natural at all. In fact, she took me off the payroll for a week and made me go into her office (I made sure to look suitably grave.) for a dressing down. Seems the company frowns deeply on one's missing one's flight. That is, if a company can, in very fact, frown.

Best wishes, m'dear – MC and HNY
Love, Chris

January 3, 1962

Happy New Year, Mom and Dad –

Ever so many thanks for the check – you are absolutely top notch parents! So glad to hear you got my package with your Christmas presents on time. Hope you had a First Class (airline speak) holiday. Mine was predictable – everyone trying too hard to be all jolly and full of good cheer. Kind of put me in a bah humbug mood.

In re my living at the beach, I fear the honeymoon is over. I didn't know this before I moved here, but apparently the weather is nice only in the summer months – the rest of the year the beaches are cold and foggy. Lately it has been sunny only about every fourth day. However, Christmas Eve was gorgeous – 80 degrees – and, get this, there were crazy beachgoers actually swimming in the icy Pacific Ocean! I'm assuming they were tourists.

I'm flying to SFO and Denver this month. The trips aren't bad, but I don't have much time off. On the days I do have off, I've been doing a bit of quasi cooking. I've been focusing on steaks – trying to get the timing just right – not an effortless task, is it? Jenny's boyfriend said the other night, "Why don't you just buy them burned?" I guess perhaps he assumed some measure of competence on my part.

Speaking of which, I would love to have some of your recipes, mom. Maybe the ones for goulash, chili and deviled eggs? And any other tantalizing delicacies you can think of – that wouldn't, of course, over tax my meager abilities.

Uh oh, I believe I detect a hunger pang

Love, Love, Love –
Christine
P.S. I was asking my flying partner last month what she thought I should buy you for Christmas, since you already have everything. She suggested, "a burglar alarm."

January 3, 1962

Hi, Mrs. Mary –

I can't truthfully say that my New Year's Eve was a disaster, but it will do until a real one comes along. Since I had no plans for the evening, I recklessly accepted an invitation to go for drinks and dinner with a passenger from my flight. He turned out to be perfect – in the sense that he was perfectly dreadful. Actually, he was kind of nice looking – in a bald sort of way. Which meant that he had no dandruff – no place to put it.

The drinks-before-dinner portion of the evening seemed to go on for several eons. Once he set a thought in motion, there was no stopping it. He had a tendency to glom onto ideas and suck them dry. In the spirit of good will toward men I nodded and made sounds of agreement now and then as he croaked on and on and on, as though he were getting paid by the word. He was a megaphone on two legs. He had opinions on everything and had no qualms about letting the world in on them. I believe I've heard this phenomenon referred to as verbal incontinence.

At one point he picked up his glass and emptied it, ignoring the fact that it held nothing. Later on he had another go at it, and was no luckier that time. On a whole, he had all the charm of a bedsore.

Your ever faithful and obedient servant – Chris
P.S. Remember back in college when you and I used to have all those earth-shaking, mind-boggling, stay-up-and-talk-all-night conversations about time and space and the universe, and why we are here, and if we are here at all, etc.? And then after a lot of beers we thought we had it all figured out? Well, the other day I read the best aphorism (is that the right word?) – it goes like this: 'Time exists so everything doesn't happen all at once; space exists so everything doesn't happen to you." Brilliant, huh?

January 20, 1962

Dear M and D –

It was with acute pleasure that I learned about Ann giving birth to her third little cherub. I trust that she and baby Kelly are both well and thriving. Boy, for sisters, we couldn't be more unalike, huh? I suppose I'll be expected to weigh in with a present at some point, which I will happily do – it gives me an excuse to go to FAO Schwartz and play with all the toys.

I went to see a CPA today about having my income tax done – he's a guy that lots of crew members use, because he knows all the ins and out. Apparently, I will get a bunch of $ back from the IRS, because just scads of expenses are deductible for airline crew members – like the cleaning and laundering of uniforms, transportation to and from the airport, and lots more stuff that I wouldn't have thought of. He's going to charge $25 or $30, but I guess it's worth it.

In case you are consumed with curiosity, JoBeth and I have decided to go to Jamaica on our vacation next month, for lack of a compelling reason to go anywhere else, and also because JoBeth wants to. It will be my first time out of the country (except for Tijuana, which I don't think really counts). We can get there for $34 round trip, and the hotels all give airline employees reduced rates. We of the nouveau poor will be looking for a no-star hotel.

Adventure beckons!

Love, Love, Love –
Christine

January 20, 1962

Hey, Mary –

Jenny is in Las Vegas today – getting married. Some people would say she was nipped in the bud. I'm one of those people.

And, our landlord is being rawther (he's English) difficult about the rent – he says we have to give him 30 days' notice before we vacate Sandy Manor. And to complicate things, my transfer to SFO could come through any day. So, we've decided that Jenny and her new helpmate will live in Sandy Manor, and I will stay with JoBeth until we move.

Did I tell you that after we have flown two years on Domestic, we are eligible to transfer to New York and fly International (to Europe)? But, before I can do that, I will have to be able to pass a test in one of the foreign languages of the countries we fly to (or rather I should say, "to which we fly," so as not to rudely conclude my sentence with one of those annoying little prepositions). That's my long-term plan anyway, so in the meantime I'm taking Spanish lessons at the airport – one hour a day and free.

When it comes to remembering any words at all from high school or college Spanish classes, my mind is a vacuous void.

That's all from the Western Front.

Love,
Chris

February 17, 1962

Dear Folks –

Oh, joy! Our transfers came through today, and we have to be in SFO on the 26th! I'm living with JoBeth until then – at Upsand Downs in Santa Monica. Now that I'm actually getting out of Dodge, I'm not sure I want to. Someone told me it's very windy in San Francisco. I really hate the wind.

I'm on reserve the rest of the month in L.A., but there are 50 of us on reserve, and apparently February is the slowest month of the year travel wise (probably the reason we got February for our vacations), so I should have only one more trip out of L.A. after this one. I'm in Dayton now – it's really a quiet town – in fact, my flying partner says it's almost unconscious.

Our vacation to Jamaica was heavenly – did you get my post card? We really enjoyed the gorgeous weather, friendly people, etc. I returned home with a sunburn and 45 cents in my pocket.

I'm in what JoBeth refers to as a "state of reduced vitality, so I will toddle off to bed now to partake of some of nature's sweet restorer (cool phrase, huh? I read it somewhere). All my love (apply as needed) -

Christine

February 17, 1962

Yo, Mary –

Soooooooooooooo wish you had been with us on our vacation. We were in Montego Bay, Jamaica, which has a gorgeous beach (not as gorgeous as Ft. Lauderdale, of course) where we spent 99% of our time. The locals were very friendly, in fact, one of them asked me out while standing on the beach with one finger up his quite sizeable nose. That scene will stay with me for the rest of my life.

One lovely tropical evening, in search of romance and adventure, we went to a club (recommended to us by finger-up-nose) called The Lemon Tree. When we walked in the door, one of the owners came rushing over to us, saying this was no place for ladies, whereupon she whisked us to a table up on the balcony, which surrounded the ground floor. Thus we had front row seats for a spectacle that was right out of a movie – local girls in skimpy dresses dancing around or draped over the bar or over drunken sailors, who were getting into fights with drunken local guys – or with each other. Another unforgettable scene.

One thing I want to warn you about, Mary, if and when you go to another country. Apparently, other countries have different electrical systems, so you need to have a thing called an adapter for anything you plug into the wall, such as a hair dryer, for instance, like the one I plugged into the wall and turned on, and then made a big loud explosion and threw me across the room. And destroyed itself. What a shock! Literally!

Love,
Chris

February 25, 1962

Dear Mother and Daddy –

Looking back at it now, I stand firm in my conviction that it was not my fault – at least not ALL my fault. The incident did, however, reinforce the fact that, sure enough, two objects cannot occupy the same space at the same time. An auto accident will never fail to bring that fact home forcefully.

JoBeth and I are in San Francisco now – we got here last night and are staying at the Bellevue Hotel. So, this morning we rented a car and set out to go apartment hunting, and before we got very far, our Audi collided with another car at what is known as an "uncontrolled intersection." We were the car on the right, so naturally I felt that I should have had the right-of-way, don't you think?

This will explain my hieroglyphic-like handwriting. My right wrist has a big bump on it, and it hurts a lot. Jo Beth had a couple of minor injuries.

So, I guess we will rent another car tomorrow and set out again, hoping for more advantageous results.

Love, Love, Love –
Christine

February 25, 1962

Hi, Mary—

Disaster strikes! JoBeth and I are in San Francisco now, staying in a hotel and looking for an apartment. Today we rented a car for just that purpose, and we weren't at it for long before — at an uncontrolled intersection — I ran into the rear end of Rear Admiral Cooke. It was nobody's fault, really, except maybe mine because I actually ran into him.

Our poor Audi was really smashed up. Possibly not useable again. Ever.

JoBeth had a cut chin and a hurt knee, so she called a doctor to come to our room, and while he was examining JoBeth, she said why didn't he look at my wrist, which hurt a lot and had a big bump on it. He felt it and said it's probably broken, so I have to go into his office tomorrow and have an X-ray and probably a cast, which will mean I can t work for a while and will have more time to get settled in and get to know the city before I start working. YAY!

Love,
Chris
P.S. JoBeth says today is just "part of life's rich pageant."

March 30, 1962

Dear Mom and Dad –

A "thank you" seems woefully inadequate for everything you did for me during the month I was at home. It was so nice to be able to spend some time with you two while my arm was in a cast. It was a lovely interval for rest and reflection. And for no work.

When I got back to San Francisco last night, JoBeth was here, along with our new roommate Dyan. She is an English girl, so she uses some unusual expressions – she calls our apartment our "flat," and she calls nail polish "nail varnish," a phone booth is a "call box," and she says "ta" for thank you and, "Oh, crikey!" or "Oh, blimey" for Oh, dear! She calls chips "crisps," French fries are "chips," and cookies are "biscuits." She has a boyfriend whose name is Bert, but she pronounces it "Butt." (She says she goes back to the U.K. every so often to renew her accent.) And, she drinks Pimms Cup, which I had never heard of, but which is quite tasty. She flies for Flying Tigers, which is a non-scheduled airline, so her trips are totally different from ours. They are mainly over the Pacific, but they could be to anywhere in the world. When she leaves on flight, she doesn't know where all she will go or how long she will be gone. BUT, they make barrels of $ - up to $900 a month! She says she always wanted to fly, ever since she was a little "gull." We sat up talking until 3:00 A.M. Dyan said we had "a jolly decent chin wag."

Today I went down to the Railway Express office to claim all my worldly goods and chattels that I had shipped from L.A. It cost $40.90, and they are going to deliver them tomorrow. Then I went to the doctor, and he took off my cast! My arm isn't any skinnier than the other one and has no long black hairs as I feared. Looks normal except the skin is all peeling off, and it's still pretty sore, so I won't be able to work for two more weeks (boo hoo). Tonight my roommates and I are having a "toddy" to celebrate the fact that I can once again bend my elbow.

Love, Love, Love –
Christine

March 30, 1962

Hello to my newly wedded Mary –

You just can't possibly imagine how wonderful it was to hear your voice via Bell Telephone, while I was at my parents' house, sponging off them and spending most of every day quivering with self-pity. Your voice was just the tonic I needed to pep me right up. I'm back on track again and will soon be ready to jump right in there and do battle with the traveling hordes.

It was really fun to be a passenger for a change on my flight back to San Francisco. The flight was, however, about 100 years too long. Just as I was settling into seat 10A, 10B comes right in, sits right down, and starts talking about himself, apparently an inexhaustible subject. Of all the seats on all the flights to all the cities of the world, he had to sit in this one. I realized that I was dealing with an inferior grade of human being when he said to the Asian girl seated on the other side of him, "Are you ornamental?" Whereupon, I immediately donned my eye mask, jammed in my ear plugs and feigned sleep for the rest of the flight.

As we deplaned in SFO, he was still holding forth.

Love,
Chris

April 20, 1962

Dear Folks –

In the Not So Good News Department: Turns out I'm getting only $75 back from my income tax. I was expecting tons more. Bugger!

In the Hurl-Your-Cap-in-the-Air News Department: I'm now a full-fledged Kelly Girl! Which means that on the days I'm not up in the air tending to the multitudes, I'll be working as a stenographer. It's just dictation and typing – nothing that requires more than a few brain cells – and I make $2 an hour. (A slightly better alternative to standing on the corner holding a cupful of pencils, don't you think?) So, all those endless hours I spent in high school learning to type and take shorthand are finally paying off. I worked Wednesday and Thursday afternoons and seven hours today, so I made $30 (before taxes) this week, which will come in mighty handy. I fly the next three days, and then for the three days after that I will play Jane Office Girl again. Before long maybe, with a modicum of effort, I will be able to trade in my sow's ear for a silk purse.

The jobs are always right downtown San Francisco, so I can take the cable car, which stops just a block from our apartment. (Did I tell you that the first few days I lived here I couldn't get to sleep until midnight, when they stop running, because of the racket from the cable car tracks? I never really got used to it, but I got used to not getting used to it.)

I'm getting to know the city a little better but still haven't met any interesting guys – I'm beginning to feel not unlike a wallflower.

Love, Love, Love –
Christine

Aprill 20, 1962

Hi, Mary –

Did you know that there are seven women for every man living in San Francisco? Well, it has become painfully evident to me lately. JoBeth and Dyan both have boyfriends here in the city, and they are either snuggled up on our couch or out cavorting every night, so I'm beginning to feel – not lonely, exactly, but dare I say – sort of, almost, slightly – left out?

The three of us went to a bar the other night that was called The Library (for no discernible reason). Every table has a telephone on it, and when someone else in the room calls your table, you have to try to figure out who it is calling you. I met a few guys that way – all distinctly inferior specimens of manhood. The first one was a flyweight named Jake, and he was very flakey – literally. He would have been well advised to consult a good dermatologist. Then came an Aussie bloke, all dressed in hit-man black, who told me that I was, "a fine bit o' goods." Then there was the hulking mass that was Al, who suggested within the first half hour of our date that we get a hotel room. I suggested that he drop dead.

I think it was W. C. Fields who said, "If at first you don't succeed, try, try again. Then give up. There's no use being a damn fool about it."

Love,
Chris

May 1, 1962

Dear Mom and Dad –

Mayday! Mayday! Just kidding – nothing's wrong – I just couldn't help myself cuz it really is May Day today.

Well, between flying and being a Kelly Girl, I've been working seven days a week. The only time I catch up on sleep is on layovers. But, what a delightful feeling it is to be solvent again! Now I can throw away my pencils and give up my spot on the corner at Union Square. Ha Ha

I'm flying to St. Louis this month, but I got balanced on a Pittsburgh flight today. To be balanced means that Scheduling sticks you on an extra trip to get as many hours as they can out of you – up to 73 hours a month, after which we get paid overtime. Some girls bid high time to make more $, but it is out-of-sight impossible to hold one of those bids when one is as low on the totem pole as I am. Hence, Kelly Girls.

I met a cute guy on the cable car the other day. I was sitting there staring out into space, when he turned to me and said, "Come down out of the clouds – you're scaring the birds." Am I going to go out with him? The answer is a resounding yes or no. After we exchanged platitudes, I gave him my number. Watch this space for further developments.

Love, Love, Love –
Christine

May 1, 1962

Hi, Mary –

In your last letter you asked how it is decided where we fly to and how often and what position we work on the airplane. Here's how it works:

Every month Scheduling publishes a list of all the flight pairings, which are numbered, and we bid for them and are awarded a schedule for that month according to our seniority. For instance, a pairing would be to fly to New York every Monday and come back every Wednesday that month. So, some girls bid to fly a lot and make extra $ flying overtime, and some bid to fly less to have more days off. And, of course, everyone bids for particular days off, like Christmas, special occasions, etc. And obviously, some cities are more desirable layover-wise than others – for instance, New York or Los Angeles as opposed to Dayton.

On the airplane the most senior girl (the one who has been flying the longest) chooses the position she wants to work, and on down the line. I usually get leftovers, because virtually everyone is senior to me.

As it stands, we have to retire when we reach age 32, so in about 10 years from now I'll be able to have all the holidays off, of which some of my personal favorites are: Groundhog Day, Washington's Birthday, Birthington's Washday, Bat Cave Cleaning Day, Fold an Origami Squid Day, The Day of the Seventh Tibia, Take a Gnat to the Oculist Day, Drink More Rice Beer Day, Use More Semicolons Day, and last but least, Throw a Peachpit at a Chihuahua Trainer Day.

Love,
Chris

May 26, 1962

Dear Mother and Daddy –

Looks like I will probably be flying reserve next month, as there are only 140 bids, and I am number 150. But, that means there will be oodles of girls on reserve – consequently, I should have eons of time off – to do what, I don't know, except to work at Kelly Girl jobs, I suppose. Or to have long bouts of lethargy and self-indulgence. The prospect doesn't cause me to leap out of bed with joy every morning.

My roommates' boyfriends have been logging considerable hours in our living room in the evenings, but I don't mind really, because they never stay very late. They are both stock brokers – or something like that – so, when the market opens in NYC (8:30, I think?), they have to be at their desks pretty early here in SFO, like 5:30. I think.

To keep up the tradition of naming our apartments, we've agreed to call this one Upin Arms. The significance of which totally escapes me. One of the best things about our apartment is the location – it's on Nob Hill – on a corner. It consists of the whole second floor of what seems to have been a big old house. It's quite spacious – big bedroom, big living room, big dining room, and big kitchen, the latter in which I have had no real successes yet – but no catastrophes, either.

Love, Love, Love –
Christine

May 26, 1962

Dear Mary –

I think the God of Dating has finally heeded my prayers – or, more likely, my complaints. A cute young man has just entered my orbit. "Young" being the key word here – he's just out of college. His name is Jim, and he's 6 feet tall with a grin just like Dobie Gillis'. We have a date for Wednesday night. I'm willing to date Babycakes at least until someone less unsuitable comes along. This may be just the thing to get my ego back in the shape God intended.

My roommate Dyan says I should expect the worst – so that I won't be disappointed. Interesting concept, huh? That 7-women-for-every-man-in-SFO statistic does not bode well – for the 7 of us. Maybe I'll have to take up some other hobby. Or move somewhere else.

Turns out it is very windy here. I hate wind. And very hilly. Which is supposedly good for the thighs. Now, if the wind could just sort of blow you up the hills, it would work out fine.

As Columbus said when he left for the New World, "Ciao."

Love,
Chris
P.S. Don't just sit there on your hands – write!

June 14, 1962

Hi, Mom and Dad –

I was absolutely thrilled to get your letter saying that you are coming to San Francisco to see me after you go to the Seattle World's Fair. Let me know exactly what days you will be here, and I will try to get some time off without having to feign sickness and go off schedule. It is my firm intention to show you everything – Fisherman's Wharf, China Town, the Golden Gate Bridge, Top of the Mark, cable cars, and on and on.

The TWA flight engineers are threatening to go on strike, but the date keeps being deferred, so I'm not too worried about it. If we should get laid off, it will be nice to have the Kelly Girl jobs to keep me right in there among the toiling masses. Also, I heard that we get unemployment compensation after the first week. Tra la.

You know, mom, I'm wishing I had let you teach me how to knit before I left home. I recently bought a HowTo Knit Yourself a Sweater book and some yummy butter yellow yarn. So, I sat right down and started in knitting and perling, and it was so fun that I just kept knitting and perling and knitting and perling for many days until the thing seemed long enough to be a sweater, but then I didn't know how to put the pieces together, so I sewed them on the sewing machine I've been renting. I don't quite understand how this happened, but the sleeves are about five inches longer than my fingertips, and the bottom hangs down - almost to my knees. Hmmmm......

No other calamities to report.

Love, Love, Love,
Christine

June 14, 1962

Hi, Mary –

Today at my Kelly Girl job I worked for an investigator who used to be an F.B.I. agent. The address I got from KG turned out to be his apartment, and when I got there I noticed that there was no one else there but the two of us. Alone. By ourselves. Now, all my other jobs have been in regular-type offices, so this was a first. Well, he took his time dictating a couple of reports, all the while staring at me, and then he took off his jacket and announced that he was going to retire to the next room, take off his clothes, and have a nap. Well, thought I to myself – uh oh – what if this gets all personal and awkward and icky. So, I immediately rolled up my sleeves, spat on my hands (so to speak) and got right down to typing those reports, lickity split – and hustled right out of there and right home to the relative safety of Upin Arms.

In retrospect, I guess he was in very fact just taking a nap, but when those red flags rear their scary little heads (can flags rear their heads?), one must sit up and pay strict attention, no?

We small town girls can't be too careful when we come across these big city guys with their smooth-talking ways.

Love,
Chris

July 25, 1962

Dear Mother and Daddy –

I have nothing of import to impart. Except to tell you that you have featured prominently in my thoughts since your visit here to San Francisco. It was so good to actually lay eyes on you both again – I really enjoyed all the things we did together. Hope this letter finds you safely at home with all your purchases intact. Were you able to get the shell jewelry box from Fisherman's Wharf and the Ming tree from Chinatown home unscathed? Tell me you did.

During my last layover in Philadelphia I wore the new dress you bought me at that shop near the Buena Vista – and was showered with compliments – I felt like a prom queen. Thanks, again.

It is with undiminished determination that I'm taking another stab at the yellow sweater project, hoping for a more appropriate size this time around. It was kind of fun ripping it out.

Tha – tha – tha – that's all folks!

Love, Love, Love –
Christine

July 25, 1962

Dear Mary –

Going on the assumption that you are dying to hear about my new love interest in Philadelphia, I feel compelled to write to you about Dennis. He's 26, has a little white MG (!), he smokes a pipe, and he has a huge schooner that he charters out to people. And, best of all, he is incredibly funny! He keeps me absolutely vibrating with laughter. For instance, when I asked him if he liked animals, he said, "Yes, they're very tasty." Then he told me this one: Confucius say, "He who flies upside down have crackup." Hahahaha – I just love him. The game is afoot!

While my flying partner and I were sitting at the pool the other day on a layover, there were two little kids playing in the kiddy pool, and I overheard one kid say to the other, "Are you a boy or a girl?" So, the other one says, "I'm three and a half." So, the first kid says, "Yeah, but are you a boy or a girl?" And, the other one says, "I have a sister." So, the first one says, "Yes, but are you a boy or a girl?" So the other one, all frustrated says, "I don't KNOW!"

Isn't that a scream?

Love, Chris
P.S. I just finished reading **Daisy Miller** – I think you would really like it. It's by Henry James, who is apparently the brother of William James (remember William James's Pragmatism from our Philosophy class? Me, neither).

Later –
Chris

August 11, 1962

Dear Folks –

Another roommate bites the dust! Looks as though next month JoBeth and her helpmate-to-be will be plighting their troth (troths?). I'll miss The Toothpick a lot – I haven't known her long, but so much has happened to us in the last six months that we agree it seems like we've been through a war together.

This brings up the problem of replacing her – roommate wise. Dyan and I could move out of Upin Arms and find a new place for two, but on the other hand there is a distinct possibility that Judy, one of my dear friends from college, may be moving here, which would work out really well. I fervently hope she does, because she's a world-class fun lover.

I've finally found someone in this city to date. His name is Ron, and although he is not a brilliant scholar, and in spite of his Neanderthal Man forehead and his Groucho Marx-like walk, he is very sweet and attentive. It's sort of an interim dating situation. I suspect he will have a shelf life of about six months. He's not "built to last."

I did meet a guy in Philadelphia recently who is over-the-top good looking. The game is afoot!

Love, Love, Love –
Christine

August 27, 1962

Oh! Oh! Oh, Mary! I'm wildly in love again! His name is Brad, and he lives in Philadelphia and is 25 and plays chess and reads good literature and likes classical music and was in the Navy but is in college now and has been indeed favored by the gods when it comes to appearance. Of all the guys I've ever dated he is #1 in looks – also, #2 through 10. He looks sort of like - no, very much like - Alan Bates. He's just made to order! I met him through another hostess, and we double dated once, and then my last trip he met me at the airport, and we spent the whole layover together.

Picture this: It was the most incredibly beautiful afternoon in the history of the world. Brad and I were strolling barefooted through a lovely wooded area in the park. The sun was sparkling, the birds tweeting, the flowers reeking. I was feeling quite enchanting in a lavender-and-white-checked summer frock – with a fitted bodice and full skirt. We ambled over a pretty little brook and then, spotting a lovely, huge old oak tree, we arranged ourselves cozily under it. At that moment Brad said something very endearing to me. I didn't reply immediately, not so much because I was trying to be coy but because at that very moment, as I drew in a breath I swallowed a fly.

Successfully proving, once again, that there are endless ways of embarrassing oneself.

Love,
Chris

September 28, 1962

Dear Folks –

I've been remiss in letting so much time go by before answering your last two letters. I crave your pardon.

Had another bit of luck earlier this month – I flew a trip to St. Louis that left on August 31 and was scheduled to return on September 2, but we got an extra day in St. Louis, because September 2 was Sky Shield Day. Now, you are no doubt saying to yourselves, "What the heck is Sky Shield Day?" The way it was explained to me was that on that day, all commercial and private aircraft were grounded, and Air Force training jets flew the scheduled routes, so that traffic controllers could practice landing them under attack conditions. It's a NORAD-run test of defense against Soviet attack. Exciting, huh?

Had a trip to New York this week where I rendezvoused with Susanne and Katy, my roommates in training. They are toying with the idea of transferring to SFO – wouldn't that just be too cool?

Went to Travis Air Force Base with a TWA pilot last Saturday night to see Stan Kenton. I really loved him. (Stan Kenton – not the pilot.)

I'm maintaining my usual routine – work/play/work/play/work/play. I wouldn't call it a rut so much as a well-oiled routine.

Love, Love, Love –
Chris

October 8, 1962

Hi, Mary –

Do you remember Phil, my old boyfriend from college? Well, we've been in touch off and on since I started flying. I had a layover in St. Louis last weekend, so he drove down from Iowa to meet me. His car, by the way, is a little red MG, which he loves passionately. Wouldn't surprise me if he French kisses it, takes it out to dinner, and sleeps with it. Oddly enough, he is a very poor car parker. It ends up looking like he has not so much parked the car as abandoned it.

Anyway, after we greeted and kissed and how-are-youd a while, we went out to dinner. Then, I'm not sure how it happened or why, but we drove across the river to East St. Louis and somehow ended up in a jazzy club that had entertainment in the form of really gorgeous women, heavily made up, exquisitely coiffed, wearing fantastic sexy costumes, who were singing and dancing on stage to all the old favorites.

We first realized that something was amiss when they were singing, "East Side, West Side," and when they came to the part that should have been "boys and girls together," they sang "boys and boys together." Turns out it was a gay club, and Phil and I were so – shall I say "out of it" – that we didn't even get the picture. It was one of those forehead-slapping revelations.

What a gas!

Love,
Chris

October 31, 1962

Hi, Mother and Daddy –

My cup well and truly runneth over! Not only did my old college buddy Judy move here to San Francisco, but Suzanne, my roommate in training, transferred here and arrived three days ago! I'm sure the paltry male population of this city will be ecstatic to find that they have two more such excellent choices at their disposal (so to speak). So, the four of us are looking for a two-bedroom apartment somewhere nearby – here on Nob Hill.

I have a great schedule for next month – I'm flying to New York City with lots of time off at home (none at Thanksgiving, however), and I'll be flying with The Toothpick. Did I tell you she got married last month? Dyan and I went to her wedding, and of course, we did the obligatory crying and weighing in with the customery presents. They rented a car and drove to Monterey for their honeymoon.

And lived happily ever after.

Love, Love, Love –
Christine

October 31, 1962

Hi, Mary –

I feel fairly certain that you have been keeping right up to date on world affairs, while I, on the other hand, keep up in a sort of theoretical sense. This may explain my astonishment, while on a layover in St. Louis last week, when a man I was having drinks with told me that there were actually – at that very moment – Soviet missiles in Cuba aimed at the U.S. and that St. Louis was one of the cities targeted. Silence supervened, while the gravity of the situation sunk into my gin-gimlet-softened brain. But, after arriving at the firm conviction that there was nothing we could do about it, we had another drink and moved on to gossip and other, lighter topics of mutual interest.

Last week a cousin of Jenny's called me – he was here on vacation from Chicago – so we went out to dinner and then to the Jazz Workshop to see Max Roach and then to the Hungry I to see Peter, Paul and Mary. The cousin is a very hairy mammal, but I don't necessarily find that unattractive.

Thrill a minute!

Love,
Chris
P.S. Have you read *The Chapman Report* by Irving Wallace? It's all the rage now.

November 29, 1962

Dear Folks –

I suspect this is going to be another of those yay/boo letters. Next month I'm flying the same New York City trip that I'm flying this month. It has good time off (yay), but unfortunately the time off is December 10 - 16, and there is only one day off at Christmas, so I won't be able to come home over the holidays (boo). I do have one pass left that has to be used before January 15 (yay), but, alas, I haven't been able to afford anything resembling a vacation (boo), so I could use it to come to see you on December 10 – 16, if that meets with your approval (yay). For a pass to go unused would be the most heinous of crimes (boo). Okay – enough of the yay/boos.

Yes, Ann wrote me that she is expecting again – she sure is taking the Bible seriously when it says to "go forth and multiply." I was thinking about getting their boys ice skates for Christmas, but Ann writes me that Kenny, who is five, wears Size 1, and Kevin, who is two, wears a 9 ½. Does that make sense to you? I don't get it.

You know how Abraham Lincoln has always been my all-time hero? Apropos of that, I had a trip to Washington, D.C. recently, so on our layover we took a tour of the White House, and then we went to the Abraham Lincoln Museum (which is the old Ford Theater where he was shot) and then to the house across the street, where he was taken after he was shot. It was really an emotional experience for me to stand in the very room where he died.

Love, Love, Love –
Christine

November 29, 1962

Hey, Mary –

When I learned that I was going to have to fly on Thanksgiving this year, I was dismayed (also pissed off), but actually I found it such a pleasant experience that I've changed my whole outlook on flying on holidays in general. First of all, there were scarcely any SOBs (souls on board, in airlinespeak) traveling on the actual holiday, so with such a light load, we couldn't really consider what we were doing as falling into the category of "work." By not having to spread ourselves so thin (so to speak) we had plenty of time to chat with everyone on an individual basis, which it turns out can be a lot of fun. Also, the passengers felt sorry for us for having to work on a holiday, so for once they didn't look upon us as cruel tyrants when we asked them to fasten their seat belts. (Yes, we admonished them – you have to fasten the seatbelt on each and every leg of the flight – not just the first one.)

Did I tell you that Suz and I are planning to transfer to New York in the spring to fly International? I'm not that keen on living in New York, but it will be worth it to fly to Europe. Before we can go to International training, we will have to pass a test in some language of one of the countries that we fly to. (Yes, we do fly to England, but no, English doesn't count.) So, I bought a Spanish book, and I'm brushing up on my meager Espanol, and I plan to go to night school in January to take Intermediate Spanish. Last night I met a really nice guy who goes to U of Calif. who speaks Spanish because his father was born in Argentina, although he is actually Irish. His name is Jaime (pronounced Hi-Me). I'm counting on free Spanish lessons.

Hasta Luego (until later) –
Chris

December 3, 1962

Hi, Folks –

Just a quickie to let you know that Phil, my old boyfriend from college, wants to drive over from Iowa to meet my flight at O'Hare on the 11th and drive me down to your house. Working on the assumption that he will be staying with us, I do want to make sure you are not averse to that plan.

Now, I know you don't do things by half, Mom, so I implore you not to go to a lot of trouble. He will be content just to sit in front of the fireplace and drink a molecule of Scotch with a few fragments of ice.

He says he's missed being with me – he's tired of finishing his own sentences.

Love, Love, Love,
Christine

December 3, 1962

Mary –

News Bulletin! JoBeth – alias The Toothpick – is pregnant already! (As Dorothy Parker once said, "I knew she had it in her.") JoBeth is ecstatic. She says that flying has been good training for when she has the baby – she's learned to survive on three hours' sleep.

We're flying together this month, and in our hotel room on layovers she walks around in the nude (yuk!), showing off her new, albeit rudimentary boobs. She has not the remotest acquaintance with shame.

She talks incessantly about BABIES, BABIES, BABIES. (Yuk!) Apparently, she feels that I rely on her extensively for this type of information. Far be it from me to try to fathom the workings of the expectant mother's mind.

Gotta flee –
Chris

January 12, 1963

Hi, Folks –

Ever so many thanks for all the gifts and $ you gave me for Christmas. As you might have imagined, the Christmas cookies and fudge that I brought back were not here in residence for long, as they were met by my roommates with lots of smiles and drooling salivary glands. It was wonderful to see you – if only fleetingly. So sorry I couldn't linger longer at home, but, as you know, I had to get back to the business of earning the three squares a day.

Had an eventful trip back from your house. About an hour this side of Chicago, Phil's adorable little red MG broke down, so we got out on the highway and thumbed a ride to the nearest toll station where we called his mom, who showed up in due time – then off we bounced to O'Hare in her Jeep, leaving her with the MG and the tow truck.

Then while waiting for my flight to SFO to board, TWA regretfully informed us that we would be delayed "an hour or so" due to traffic. After waiting "an hour or so," we boarded the plane and then were regretfully informed that there was something wrong with one of the plane's engines and that we would have to wait for another airplane to come and take us. After waiting several years, the alternate airplane did arrive, collected us, and delivered us to SFO - arriving about 1:00 AM. I was home and in bed by 3:30 – up again at 5:30 to work a flight to New York, where I dove headlong into bed and slept for 14 hours.

Such a glamorous life!

Love, Love, Love –
Christine

January 12, 1963

Hey, Mary –

Feliz Nuevo Ano (or *Feliz Ano Nuevo* – I'm not sure). Think I told you I'm boning up on my pitiful Espanol in hopeful expectation of flying International in the summer.

Have you ever been so physically tired you couldn't get buzzed no matter how many drinks you had? Happened to me on – of all nights – New Year's Eve! I went off schedule to be home for that night, but Judy and I had to spend that day moving into our new apartment (a two bedroom for the four of us). The other two roomies were out on flight that day, so that left it up to Judy and me to tote all the belongings just two blocks, but up a very steep hill. We had some help in the form of a couple of friends of the masculine persuasion – actually, our dates for New Year's Eve.

So, after patting ourselves on the back for getting it all done in record time, we got dressed up and went to a party, and subsequently found ourselves just sort of standing around, all glassy eyed – four total party poopers – not up to the obligatory jollity.

The pity of it was that my date was a real cutie – blond, 6 feet tall – an aeronautical engineer from Arkansas. But, try as we might, we just couldn't work up any enthusiasm. *Que triste.*

No telephone here yet - it's supposed to surface within the week.

Adios –
Chris

February 28, 1963

Dear Mother and Daddy –

Celebrating Mardi Gras in New Orleans, whatever you've heard about it, is not an experience worth repeating. Suz and I got back last night from doing just that. I'm not saying Mardi Gras was disappointing. It was, but that's not what I'm saying. I'm saying it was really disgusting – lots of college kids bent on consuming all the beer in Louisiana, staggering around the streets throwing up, getting into bloody fights, and passing out in the gutter. It was only due to our adroit footwork that we were barely able to avoid being splattered with blood and vomit. (We had the distinct feeling that we had fallen among savages.) And the parades were barely second-rate. Suz ventured to say that a few well-aimed grenades would have made the world a better place.

We were there three days – then stopped in Las Vegas on the way back and saw Robert Goulet and Myron Cohen (separately) at the Flamingo.

You'll no doubt be pleased to learn that I spent the $ you gave me for Christmas on Living Language Spanish records. I whipped through the first five lessons in the first day and am now up to Lesson 8. On a less happy note, I went to my first Spanish class at Berlitz downtown, and it was pretty intimidating – seemed like everyone in class spoke Spanish fluently. So, I slunk back home to my records with my tail between my legs. So to speak.

Love, Love, Love –
Christine
P.S. Could you send me my birth certificate? I need to get a passport.

February 28, 1963

Hola, Mary -

Como esta usted? That means, "How are you?"

Perhaps "terror-stricken" may be too strong a term to describe my emotion on a recent flight, but I don't think so. I was working a night flight to ORD – took off from SFO – got up over the city – and then started going DOWN right into the city. I really thought at that point that my hour had come. But then the seat belt sign went back on, and it turned out we just had a fire warning in one of the engines, so we had to go back and change airplanes. (Not as fast and easy as changing your socks, ya' know.)

While I would have thought I was made of sterner stuff, much to my chagrin that episode left me limp all night for the rest of the flight – couldn't even hold up my book to read (which is verboten, anyway, when you're working a flight).

This is the sort of thing I don't dare write to my folks about – my mom is a world-class worrier. She has some quaint theory that every time I take off my chances of crashing increase. But, when I tell her I have the same odds each time I take off, she takes everything I say with a grain of panic, maintaining that being up in an airplane is in open defiance of the laws of physics, anyway.

On a lighter note, we had a fun passenger on that flight – when he was deplaning in ORD, he said, "This has been fun. Next time –my place!"

Hasta Luego -
Chris

March 13, 1963

Dear Mom and Daddy –

Can it be true? Did I actually fail to explain in my last letter why I need a passport just now? I'm so intensely excited! My roommate Dyan and I have decided on Hong Kong for our first big vacation. That is, providing the $ I'm borrowing from the Credit Union arrives before my vacation does. We plan to spend a few days in Tokyo on the way over and a few days in Honolulu on the way back. So, I've been mucho busy with the tedious details of getting visas, tickets, smallpox and cholera shots and having my income tax done, whilst eking out some time to show up for work.

Can't afford to buy any new duds for the trip, but apparently the Chinese make clothes to order there – really cheaply and really fast – chop chop.

Still have my nose to the grindstone studying Spanish – and getting sort of panicky now that May is creeping up. That's the month that International opens up and people start transferring in. Suzanne decided not to fly International just now cuz she's in love with some guy here, so I guess I'll have to find someone else to live with in New York. That is, if I pass the Spanish test. Wish me *buena suerte* (good luck).

Love, Love, Love –
Christine

March 24, 1963

Hiya, Mary –
Last night I went to a Persian New Year's Eve party – with a guy named Jacob, who is, as you might have guessed, from Persia. Now, you may be saying to yourself, and rightfully so, "New Years? In March?" Well, it turns out that their new year begins the first day of spring.

It wasn't much fun, though. In, fact, the event really didn't even fall into the category that one would label a "party." It took place in an enormous hall in the Sheraton Palace Hotel, and there were about 1,000 people there (really). We just sort of stood around drinking no alcohol. Leaving the party was far and away the high spot of the evening. I've put it on my must-miss list for next year. To quote Groucho Marx, "I've had a perfectly lovely evening, but this wasn't it."

Here's something that's been puzzling me for a while. You know those sayings, "For Pete's sake," and "By George," and "Great Scott," and "For the love of Mike?" Who the heck ARE these people? And why are we invoking them?

I bow to your superior knowledge in these matters.

Love,
Chris

April 20, 1963

Greetings Mama-san and Papa-san – *Ni Hao* (Chinese for Hello)

Arrived home last night from the Fabled East – what a fantastic trip! Hong Kong is THE MOST exciting place I've ever been (which isn't too surprising, I guess, since I've only ever been out of the country once before). Dyan and I both loved it so much that we wanted to move right in and settle down. She felt right at home, since all the non-Chinese people have the same English accent she has.

Everything there is such a huge bargain, that our meager little resources went a long way. I indulged myself in a jade ring, a jewelry box, a silk blouse and a camera. At one shop I bought a purse and a pair of shoes and had two silk dresses made – all for $44. We agreed that whatever funds we had with us would undoubtedly remain there in the capable hands of the Chinese.

One day we took the equivalent of a Greyhound bus ride to a little village up north to the New Territories, where many of the people live on sampans and have cholera. It was a beautiful ride through the mountains, and we saw people working in the rice fields and living in little shacks. Another day we had our hair done for $1 and then went to Aberdeen, which is on the other side of Hong Kong island and took a ride in a sampan out to a floating restaurant for a beer. I think the high point – literally – of the trip was when we took the cable car up to Victoria Peak – the view of Hong Kong and Kowloon was breathtaking. Our last night there our tailor took us out for a traditional Chinese dinner, where we drank green tea and learned how to use chopsticks (sort of).

We weren't overly fond of Tokyo. It was really cold there, and nobody seemed very friendly. Apparently, women (and especially Western women) are looked down on in Japan. In fact, we were denied entrance into one place and told that it was "only for Japanese," which was a real eye opener for us.

We couldn't make hotel reservations anywhere ahead of time, because our airline passes were standby, so when we arrived in Tokyo, we were told at the Tourist Desk at the airport that, because it was cherry blossom time, and thus the height of the tourist season, the only hotel room available in the whole city was in the Tokyo Tower Hotel. I suspect our room was never meant to be a hotel room – it was sort of like a garage – with a concrete floor and single naked light bulb hanging down from the ceiling on a long wire. The beds were on the floor, and everything else in the room was only about as high as our kneecaps. The rest room and bath (cold) were outside and around the corner. We were asked to leave our shoes at the door and given slippers to walk around in (presumably to keep us from ruining the concrete floor).

The next day we went up in the Tokyo Tower (TV station – highest point in the city), saw the Imperial Garden, where the emperor lives (I don't mean he lives in the garden, but it's the garden of where he lives), and participated in a traditional tea ceremony (which for them is a big deal). I picked up a few fripperies in a famous round department store on the Ginza (that's the name of the main street).

The last day we took a train to Kamakura to see the Great Buddha, which is a bronze statue, 44 feet tall, built in 1252. Then we spent that afternoon sleeping through Kabuki Theater.

After that, we spent a few days in Honolulu, where it rained all day every day except the day we left.

What a tremendous letdown to be back home to the old humdrum life.

Love, Love, Love –
Most Unworthy 2nd Daughter

April 2⁻, 1963

Ni Hao (Chinese for hello), Mary!

Dyan and I just got back from our first big vacation adventure - to the Mysterious East – namely Hong Kong and Tokyo. With a few days in Honolulu. We ADORED Hong Kong – did the usual touristy things and also spent lots of time drinking beer with other people – mostly sailors from various places around the world.

We had some clothes made, and apparently, now that they have my measurements, I was delighted to learn that I can just send the tailor a picture of a garment, and they will make it to fit me. (Dyan tells me that I have an unrivaled capacity for believing in miracles.) One day while we were in his shop, our tailor told us that he had to leave to go vote because that day was "erection" day.

In Tokyo we also did the obligatory touristy things. As you undoubtedly have noticed, the Japanese people are a little smaller than we are, and it seemed like we were constantly bumping our heads on things. I felt like a real clod. And, the Japanese women are so tiny and feminine that next to them I felt like a big old clumsy bumpkin.

We met two guys from the Philippines who were in Tokyo on business, so one night they took us out for a traditional Japanese dinner. We ate *shiba ebi, kisu, megochi, ginnan, ika, anago, nasu, kaibashira*, and other mysterious looking globules. They cooked some squirming little live eels right in front of us. Literally, a moveable feast.

It rained every day we were in Honolulu, so we spent our time productively - drinking beer. The day we were to come home, we got to the airport 45 minutes before departure, and BOAC wouldn't let us on the flight, because it's considered an international flight for them, so they closed out the flight one hour before departure. No matter HOW MUCH we cajoled and pleaded with them, it was no good. There was nothing left to do but to burst into tears. And return the following day and have another go at it.

Consequently, we arrived home just in time for me to go off schedule, because I was supposed to work a flight that night. Fingers crossed I don't get into trouble.

I had a welcome home letter from Brad saying he hopes I brought back lots of fireworks from China, so when I come to Philadelphia, we can blow up the airport and I can stay there indefinitely.

Wasn't that sweet?

Zai-Jian (goodbye) –
Chris

May 27, 1963

Hi, Folks!

I'm all a twitter! My dream of traveling the world is actually about to come true!

Since I last wrote I passed the dreaded Spanish test (applause here) and was immediately sent to Kansas City for a week of International training. There were quite a few of us from SFO there and also a few girls that I knew from basic training and from LAX. So, it was sort of like a mini reunion.

We got to fly First Class to Kansas City and back, and the training didn't unduly tax our brains, so that it was actually quite fun. I'm back home now, just sitting tight waiting for my transfer to New York to come through. Should be any day now. Adventure beckons!

Remember Katy, one of my dear roommates in basic training? Well, she's based in New York, flying International now, and - oh, lucky me! - one of her roommates is getting married and moving out, so I'll be able to move right in with them when I get there.

Whoever said, "Time flies on swift wings," was obviously not sitting around waiting for his transfer to come through.

Love, Love, Love –
Christine

May 27, 1963

Hola, Mary!

It's official! I'm moving to New York to fly International! Whoopee!

I passed the Spanish test - with a little prompting from the lady who gave the test. She was very nice, and I know she really wanted me to pass – even though I could not be made to think of the English word for "*mar*," in spite of her pointing out of the window at the water in the distance. (It's "sea," by the way.) Don't think I could have remembered it even with benefit of sodium pentothal.

I had a week's training in Kansas City, which didn't take a razor-like intelligence to get through. The atmosphere was totally the opposite of when we were there the first time and didn't know anybody and were scared witless. This time it was fun!

When I get to New York I'm going to be living in a fifth-floor walkup with two other girls – one of which is Katy, who was one of my roommates in basic training. I'm told that apartments in New York City are about twice as expensive and half as nice as they are here. And, not entirely divested of cockroaches.

A couple of flies in the ointment – I was suitably chastised and docked two days' pay for missing my flight after vacation. (My supervisor made "missed flight" sound like a deadly sin.) Also, the IRS is auditing my income tax return. Rats!

Love,
Chris

May 29, 1963

Dear Mom and Dad –

I'm enclosing a copy of a hilarious letter I just received from our tailor in Hong Kong - in reply to a picture of a dress and coat that I sent him to copy. I really don't mean to make fun of him. I can't imagine trying to get that thought – or any thought – across to him in Chinese.

Love, Love, Love –
Christine

May 29, 1963

Hey, Mary – you are going to love this – it's a copy of a letter I just got from our inscrutable Asian tailor in Hong Kong who had told me I could just send him a picture of a dress and coat, and he would make it in my size.

Later –
Chris

"May 19, 1963

Dear Mrs.

I had received your kindly letter in 28th April 1963. But I am sorry to say and so late to reply you kindly letter. Because you had very interesting for the dress and with the coat. But I am very regret for the dress and the coat that two things if to your hand could be prove the things produce from where? Much be want the certificate of origin. If you are friends come to Hong Kong that I can fix for you. Because they can bring to you and no necessary the certificate of origin. So, I am very sorry to say, may be you can buy in State. But I still waiting for your wool business. Thank you very much. And with my best regards to you and I will Always service for you

Yours truly
Frank Yuen"

June 12, 1963

Dear Folks –

Bulletin from the front: I'm now what's known as a Manhattan cliff dweller. I'm living on the upper east side in a fifth-floor walkup, with Katy, who was one of my roommates in initial training and another hostess named Ronnie, whom I have decided is one serious wackadoodle. (She's not dangerous or anything – just eccentric.) She drinks water all day – with a little Scotch in it for flavoring. I'll be flying to Lisbon for the rest of the month – once a week with a 24-hour layover, so with a little bit of luck, I won't be in residence the same time as Ronnie roommate.

I worked my first International trip last week – it was to Rome – full loads both ways, and what transpired was something very closely resembling HARD WORK. We left JFK in the evening, and when we landed in Rome it was morning, so we just stayed up – walked around the city for a while – I bought a pair of shoes - went back to the hotel and slept a couple of hours – had dinner – went to a party – got back to the hotel in time to sleep three whole hours – then worked the flight home. By the time I got back to my apartment and struggled up the four flights of stairs, I was so exhausted that I just sort of melted into my bed and slept 16 hours. Not exactly my idea of *La Dolce Vita*.

The next night Katy and I doubled with two friends of hers – FBI agents, actually, and we went to a Gershwin concert at Lincoln Center – then out to drinks and dinner in Greenwich Village.

Thrill-a-minute!

Love, Love, Love,
Christine

June 12 1963

Hey, Mary –

I would herewith like to go on record as stating that in my opinion New York City is a fine place to visit, but I wouldn't want to live there. But, I do. I'm living with Katy and another hostess named Ronnie in a fifth-floor walkup, which they seem to think is a real find, but which in my opinion doesn't have much to recommend it. The fact that we can barely see a little bit of the East River out of one of our windows is supposed to be some sort of a big deal, I guess It's an old building in an old neighborhood, and between the garbage and the dog poop on the street, the smell is too odious for the human nostril.

As for Ronnie roommate, the minute I met her she got on my nerves and stayed there. When I first walked in the door of the apartment, she was actually scrubbing the woodwork – with a maniacal look in her eye! I ask you – is that the act of a rational human being?

No roommate problems on layovers, however – on International we have single rooms! I'll be flying to Lisbon this month – as you might have guessed, they speak Portuguese there, so there is little chance that I'll be able to communicate with any of the locals. Won't hinder my shopping, though. I plan to use the age-old, time-honored point and pay method.

Ciao –
Chris

July 22, 1963

Hi, Mom and Daddy –

Much has transpired since I last wrote. As you might have predicted, I didn't stay in that last apartment long enough even to give it a name. Ronnie roommate's unflagging obsession proved to be just too much to bear – you would think she invented cleanliness. Katy and I couldn't sit still around the apartment for any length of time, lest she might decide to dust us off and shine us up. I can see the headlines now: "TWA HOSTESS MURDERS ROOMMATES – ACCIDENTALLY SUCKS OUT INNARDS WITH VACUUM CLEANER."

So, Katy and I and another hostess named Lori – who also just transferred to International from SFO and was looking for a place to live – went traipsing around town on our days off, looking for a new abode, and eventually found The Perfect Place. It's on East 54th St. – next door to El Morocco. We live on the second floor, and it has an elevator! Also, air conditioning, which is a godsend just now (thanks, Big Fella) because it's been in the 90's every day, with humidity to spare. We've named our new digs Midtown Manor.

We will have to beg, borrow, or steal – or as a last resort, buy a bunch of stuff, like dishes, silverware, pots and pans, ironing board, toaster, etc. I've decided I like moving – it's fun! The psychiatrist in me attributes it to that nest-making instinct that we all supposedly harbor.

Love, Love, Love –
Christine

July 22, 1963 –

Hi Ho, Mary –

I've decided that the most difficult part of flying International
is selling drinks in Coach. Here's how it goes: Right after
takeoff we set up the cart with all the beverage options on it,
and away we go, careening down the aisle to face the thirsty
mob, smiling and hawking our wares. Which in itself is no
big deal, but the change-making process is a tricky business,
requiring every last little cell in my brain. The passengers
present us with all kinds of money – pounds, marks, drachmas,
francs, lira, pesetas – everything but doubloons and pieces of
eight – and we are supposed to figure out how much their
drink costs in that money and give them back their change,
either in kind or in U.S. Dollars. Can you see my dilemma?
(I'll thank you for a little sympathy here, please.)

   This month I'm flying to Rome – I go out every
Thursday night and get home Saturday night. I'm flying with
my roommate Katy, which has worked out well, because that
means we've had the same days off to go apartment hunting
together. Yes, you guessed it. I lost no time at all moving out
of the fifth-floor walkup with the wonky roommate. Now
we live in a place where we can walk to everything – grocery
store, cleaners, post office, drug store, bank, Fifth Avenue,
and best of all – Bloomingdales!

   Celebrity sighting! I was in Saks the other day, and guess
who I saw? Loretta Young! She is a lovely creature.

Ciao –
Chris

August 6, 1963

Dear Mother and Daddy –

You know how intensely grateful I always am when anything resembling a bit of good luck falls my way, right? Well, I recently traded into a Paris trip - we were supposed to have the usual 24-hour layover in Paris and then work to Rome the next day. But our flight to Rome cancelled, so we had an extra day in Paris. Whoopie! The first day we were too tired to do anything but walk down the Champs Elysee to buy some *"parfum"* at Catherine's (where airline folks get a 40% discount). The next day we went to the Notre Dame Cathedral, walked around the Left Bank, took the Metro (subway) to the Louvre and saw the Mona Lisa and the Venus de Milo. That night we deadheaded to Rome, and by the time we hit the sack it was 5:00 A.M. – up at 7:00 A.M. to work the flight home. By the time I got to bed in Midtown Manor (our new apartment), I had been up 42 hours with only 2 hours of sleep. Took me two days to recover from that one.

More good news – in a few months we are going to get a whopping $40 a month raise! My joy is unbounded.

Love, Love, Love –
Christine
P.S. On my last flight I congratulated the captain on a very smooth landing, and he answered, "Any landing you can walk away from is a good landing."

August 6, 1963

Hi, Mary –

I'm flying to Rome again this month with my roommate Katy, and our last trip was *molto bello* (I think that means really fun.) When we got there it was morning, and we had been up all night working the flight, so we started out on a sightseeing tour, which normally is right up there at the top of the list of things I wouldn't be caught dead doing, but we had just worked a full load to get there, and it sounded like sort of an easy way to see a lot of sights. We stuck with it long enough to see the Appian Way, the Catacombs and some cathedrals, but when we got to the Trevi Fountain, we found we just couldn't bear careening around in the hot bus with the irritating, sweaty fellow tourists any longer, so we jumped ship and took off on our own. We had lunch on the Via Veneto, saw some other touristy stuff, bought some leather gloves (very cheap there) and some shoes (very cute and very cheap) and went back to the hotel and had dinner on my balcony in our nightgowns. Not exactly *La Dolce Vita*, but pretty close.

I've tried using some of my elementary Spanish on the locals, but they thought I was trying to speak Italian, so they just kept correcting me. Must get a phrase book.

Ciao –
Chris
P.S. I saw my wacky ex-roommate Ronnie at the airport the other day. I saw her only from a distance – the best way to see her.

September 7, 1963

Dear Mom and Dad –

In your last letter, Mom, you asked me what a purser is and what he does. We have pursers only on International flights – they are in charge of the cabin of the airplane (as opposed to the cockpit). It is the purser who is in charge of all the paperwork and all the monies. (I don't know why they are called "monies" – isn't "money" already plural?) He also sells the Duty Free items and is the one to run to if anything untoward happens. Like, for instance, on my last trip where there was a fist fight in the aisle of First Class, because apparently 2D reclined his seat suddenly and forcefully, knocking 3D's glass of red wine all over his dinner and the front of his spiffy white shirt. Whereupon, 3D got up and confronted 2D, calling him an unflattering name, so 2D got up and punched 3D in the nose, and 3D returned the favor, and that's how it went until the purser, hearing the call of battle, plunged into the fray, separating the combatants and putting an end to what had become, for us, the in-flight entertainment. A situation like this is one of the reasons the purser's duties earn him more "monies" than the rest of us.

    I'm flying to Paris this month with my roommate Lori. We leave every Sunday morning, have a 42-hour layover and come home Tuesday afternoon. *Tres jolie!* I love my job!

Love, Love, Love –
Christine

September 7, 1963

Hi, Mary –

Love life update: The other night I went out with a friend of the guy Katy is dating. We saw an off-Broadway musical, went to a couple of nightclubs and had breakfast at the Playboy Club. We went out again last night – had drinks and dinner at a Russian restaurant. I had what is called a Russian Witch – made with vodka and apple cider – very tasty – try it! We're supposed to go out again tonight, but I don't want to, so I'm not answering the phone today. I call him "the man of my dreams," in the sense that when he talks to me, I fall asleep.

Went out with the guy who lives across the hall recently. We went to Trader Vic's for dinner and then to the Plaza bar for drinks. His name is Jason – he's 30 – 6"3' and blond. I think he must have piles of $, because he has a seat on the Stock Exchange. Also, he let a few things drop, like his folks have a butler/cook person, his mother drives a T-Bird, his father always goes south for the winter, he has been skiing in Switzerland, his sister had her coming-out party at the Plaza, etc. etc. I know it's hard to imagine, but he didn't say those things in a bragging sort of way – they just came out in the conversation. He's really awfully sweet and fun. I'm smitten. The game is afoot!

Love,
Chris

October 1, 1963

Bonjour, mes Parents –
  Comment alez vous? (How are you?)
  Got back last night from the BEST trip to Paris. I was flying with my roommate Lori, and we were lucky enough to have two days there instead of the usual one. We stayed at a hotel called the Royal Monceau, which everyone calls the Royal Monster. We got up early (can you imagine that?) the first morning and went to Versailles and walked through the Palace and gardens. In the afternoon we went to the Louvre and saw Impressionist paintings – then in the evening we went to the ballet and saw Swan Lake. The next day we had our hair done, went to another ballet and then drank beer with a couple of Russian guys we met. (The bar we went to had a sign admonishing women not to have children at the bar. Apparently the hospital is still the preferred place.) All in all, a superb layover.
  Today I had the funniest thank-you note in the mail from Ann's little boy Kenny. It goes like this:
  "Dear Ant Chris –Thack you for The draing [drawing] cint [kit] it was fun hear is a pecker [picture] ofa garl [girl] I trast [traced] – It was my frafrit [favorite] So I dwoi t [drawed it].Love, Kenny"Isn't that a scream?

Love, Love, Love –
Christine

October 1, 1963

Dear Mary –

Do you remember my talking about Dick, who was my boss when I was working my way through college as a secretary? Well, we've kept in touch off and on, and he was in town recently, so we got together for dinner one night, after which I went with him up to his hotel room to see a present he had bought that day for his wife – all very innocent (really). He happened to be staying at a hotel on the west side down around Times Square, which is an area with no lack of streetwalkers and other characters of dubious reputation.

Which explains, I guess, why we weren't in the room 20 minutes before the house detective knocked on the door and politely asked me to leave, actually accompanying me down the elevator and walking me out the front door onto the street! Thus depriving me of the last of those pesky little shreds of dignity. (I think I read that last phrase somewhere, but it really did apply.)

Toooooooooooooooooooo humiliating!

Ta Ta –
Chris

October 20, 1963

Dear Folks –

If my last trip to Paris were a play, I guess it would be considered a Tragedy. I'm flying with my roommate Lori again this month, and our plan, once we got to Paris, was to have our hair done at Antoine's (very exclusive, but they give us an airline discount – wash and set for $2), then to go shopping, keeping our eyes peeled (sounds painful, huh?) for paintings to give to our parents for Christmas, and then go see *Madam Butterfly* in the evening.

As it turned out, Antoine's was closed that day, we couldn't find any paintings we could afford, and – for the *coup de grace* - the opera was sold out. There was great wailing and gnashing of teeth on our part, followed by some unladylike language before we bowed to the inevitable and repaired to the nearest bistro for a much-needed restorative – or two.

The next day we were scheduled to come home, but our flight cancelled, and we were told not to leave our hotel rooms, so we were kept sitting around wasting the whole day while Scheduling decided what to do with us. We finally came home the following day. *Cest la guerre.*

We were reminded once again of what we were told in training – that nothing in the airlines is certain – except change.

Love, Love, Love –
Christine

October 20, 1963

Dear Mary –

Congratulations!!! I can brag to all my friends now that my dear friend is a published author! And in such a prestigious magazine! How does it feel to be a bona fide writer? Will you write lots of books and become rich and famous? Will you still speak to me?

I flew with a purser my last trip who told me a story about his little boy who had just turned six years old and was so excited about being old enough to go to school. So, they bought him a brand new pencil box and a spiffy new outfit to wear, and he was so excited he could hardly sleep the night before.

They dropped him off in the morning and told him they would be back at 3:00 to pick him up after school. When they came back to pick him up, he was standing outside the school looking very sad and dejected, and when they asked him how it went, he said, "Oh, it was just fine. But they want me to come back tomorrow."

Love,
Chris
P.S. Another celebrity sighting. I was in Saks the other day, and who was standing one counter over, but Lena Horne! She's gorgeous!

November 30, 1963

Dear Mother and Daddy –

Madness reigns. Where were you when Kennedy was shot? I was in Woolworth's when the announcement came over the loud speaker. Everyone got very quiet and started moving very slowly – like we were in a trance. What a horrible loss. It's ...... beyond words.

On a lighter note, this week I got a letter from big sister Ann – here's what she said: "The kids are all outside and talking about their grandmas. Little Kenny mentioned grandma's house and Chris's room, and another little kid wanted to know who Chris is. Kenny said 'You know – THEIR Chris. She's 15 or 16.'"

More about pursers. Part of their job is to hold a "briefing" with all the cabin crew before every flight to tell us the load, the flight time, any notable passengers, and all pertinent info about the flight. Also, to have us choose the positions we work and to assign crew rest times. This month our purser is too funny. He began our first briefing by saying, "I've called you all together to name the murderer." And, at the end of the briefing he said, "Do as I say and nobody gets hurt." Hahahahahaha

Love, Love, Love –
Your Ever Youthful - Christine

November 30, 1963

Buenos Dias, Mary –

When I look back on November 22, it seems like an eerie dream. Where were you when you heard about the assassination? Like everyone else, my roommates and I were glued to the TV the whole of that weekend. Conspiracy or not? What do you think?

I'm flying to Madrid for the next two months. When I found out I could hold that line, I was really excited, thinking that now I'll get to try my pitiful Spanish on some real live Spaniards. So, on my first flight to Madrid, as we were serving dinner in coach, I asked a Spanish couple if they wanted to eat dinner, but they both just gave me really puzzled looks. I realized later that I had said to them, "Am I hungry?"

Later on in the flight another Spanish passenger said, "Excuse my pardon, please," and then asked me if he could please have "a cup of glass" (he meant a glass of ice). When I gave it to him, he said, "Thank you every much."

My latest love is a Jewish interior decorator, originally from Cuba (yet another chance to practice my fractured Spanish). He's a budding actor, also an artist and used to be a TV cameraman. He's a very sturdy looking sort of person with a face not unlike Marlon Brando. Nothing serious, though – he's poor.

Adios –
Chris

December 19, 1963

Buenos Dias, Folks –

This letter is getting itself written in Madrid – just got back to the hotel from being fitted at a tailor for a made-to-order suede jacket. I chose a gorgeous blue-green color (teal, maybe?), and my flying partner chose a luscious wine red. Besides being very inexpensive here, we got an airline discount, which makes it a real deal. Heads will swivel when we get back to New York and stroll down Fifth Ave.

The flight coming over was nearly empty. It was night, and not a creature was stirring, so I got to sit and watch the whole movie without one interruption from the inmates. The movie was *"**The Wheeler Dealers**."* Mediocre.

Don't know if I've mentioned it, but nearly all of our flights to Europe leave out of JFK in the early evening. So, while boarding this flight, one of the passengers muttered to me, "TWA – the fly-by-night airline." Ha ha

Gotta dash – I'm meeting the rest of the crew to go out to dinner to a *ristorante* called Casa Botin, which apparently first opened in 1725 (yes, that is 1725). They specialize in roast suckling pig – and tiny fresh wild strawberries for dessert. Yum!

The undersigned is looking forward mightily to coming home for Christmas.

Love, Love, Love –
Christine

December 19, 1963

Hola, Mary –

It is my painful duty to report that I took to the kitchen again recently. (As you know, I was sort of late to the party when it came to learning how to cook.) This was meant to be a surprise birthday dinner for my new Cuban paramour. He arrived just as I was putting the burnt saucepans in to soak. He said, "Oh, Chris – you shouldn't have." He was right – I shouldn't have. The smell of burnt *coq au vin* will always remind me of him. I think I'll put that whole cooking effort on the back burner. (That's either a very clever or a very terrible pun. If it's the latter, I apologize.)

We had a surprise house guest in Midtown Manor recently in the form of an enormous, brown, museum-quality cockroach. Unfortunately, he passed away during the night after a hefty Webster's dictionary mysteriously slammed on top of him and crushed him. We are hoping he didn't leave any heirs

Feliz Navidad
Adios –
Chris

January 16, 1964

Dear Folks –

Sooooo wonderful to be able to spend Christmas with you – thanx 1,000,000 for a delightful visit, and for all the lovely presents. I've really made good use of the electric blanket you gave me. I recently spent a week in bed with a cold and the flu, and since the heat here in Midtown Manor is often – you might say, "lacking in vigor," and since I had the chills, I was happy to be able to hug my new warm blanket to my shivering bosom.

Wish you could have been with me on my first trip to Frankfurt last week. When we landed it was early morning, and when I walked outside the terminal I looked up, and the tree branches were all encrusted in ice. With the sun glistening on them and the ground covered with snow, it looked like a beautiful fairyland. I'll never forget it.

We stay in Bad Homburg, which is a small town about 20 minutes on the bus from Frankfurt. Maybe you already knew this, but I've learned that "Bad" means "bath" in German. Apparently, all the towns that are named Bad something-or-other are resort areas that have mineral springs where people come for mineral baths. That first night my flying partner and I had a delicious Saurbraten dinner – then went to a gambling casino and watched people playing roulette. The next day we had our hair done and then took the bus to Frankfurt and gave ourselves over to a pleasantly self-indulgent afternoon of shopping. In the evening we saw **Madame Butterfly** in the beautiful new Frankfurt opera house. Now, obviously I'm not an expert on opera or anything, but I did find it a little weird to hear the Japanese Madame Butterfly pouring out her heart in German.

Auf Wiedersein –
Christine

January 16, 1964

Hi, Mary –

The latest stop-press news is that I'm flying to Frankfurt this month. Do you want me to buy anything for you there? I'm going to get some Hummel figurines for my mom and some Rosenthal china for myself. Certain things are much cheaper in der Fatherland than they are in the U.S., so shopping there is great sport. As you may imagine, it's bitterly cold there this time of year, so from time to time we are forced to take time out from our shopping in order to digest large quantities of stimulants. In huge steins. With lids on them.

As crew members, we are allowed to bring only $10 worth of stuff through U.S. Customs each trip, without paying duty, so I'll have to bring in one dish – or one Hummel – or one whatever – at a time, and also get a little inventive on my declaration form. My last trip the customs inspector said to me, "I'd like to have my wife take lessons from you. You airline people can buy more for $10 than anyone I know."

Auf Wiedersein –
Chris

February 27, 1964

Dear *Mutter und Vater* –

So glad to hear you received the Hummels, Mom – and even gladder to hear they arrived unbroken. I'm flying to Frankfurt again this month, if you want me to buy any more of them for you. I'm with the same crew this month as last, which is fun, because we know (sort of) and seem to like (sort of) each other by now. Since we are lucky enough to get the rare two-day layovers, we've been taking the train to other towns – Mainz and Heidelberg, so far. We wanted to fly over to Berlin for a day, but the tours of East Berlin don't start until April.

Mainz is a picturesque little town on the Rhine, and the day we were there they were celebrating Fashing (Mardi Gras), so we got to see the parade and join in the festivities. The next trip we went over to Heidelberg and walked all through the castle and saw what we were told is the biggest wine barrel in the whole world – it holds something like 58,000 gallons.

I was flying home from Frankfurt on my birthday, and would you believe that I totally forgot that it was actually my birthday until about noon? Obviously, I haven't let my brains go to my head.

Auf Weidersein –
Christine

February 27, 1964

Achtung. Mary!

As I was strolling down the street in Frankfurt the other day, a German woman approached me and asked – in German – where the *Bahnhof* was. Well, I happened to have just come from the *Bahnhof* (train station) and was still within pointing distance of it, and *Bahnhof* happened to be one of the five words I know in German, so I pointed down the street, and she smiled and *Danke schoened* me, and I smiled and *Bitte schoened* her, and she went on her way, never knowing she had been given directions by a New Yorker.

Someone told me the German word for "girdle" is "hinderbinder." I wonder. We've been having a lot of fun with German words – with the "ausfahrts" (way out) and "einfahrts" (way in) and various other fahrts. We saw a sign that said "rundfahrt," and my flying partner said, "Oh, now they come in shapes!"

Auf Weidersein –

Chris

March 15, 1964

Dear Ones –

It just occurred to me that I may have neglected to tell you about the beautiful new TWA terminal we fly out of at JFK in New York. It may take me 1,000 words to describe it, so I'll plan to send you a picture of it at some point.

The building opened in May of 1962, and it was designed by the Finnish American architect Eero Saarinen, who died in 1961. (He also designed the Gateway Arch in St. Louis.) He was known for his futuristic style, and our terminal is a perfect example. It's built out of concrete, and the roof is made up of gigantic shells made to look kind of like wings.

The inside is all curvy and spacious, with different levels. Up some stairs and straight ahead a ways and then down a few steps is a red-carpeted lounge area with floor-to-ceiling windows, slanted out at the top. Up some stairs to another level on the right is a restaurant called the Paris Café, where some of us meet and eat before we go out on flight. Then, to get to the gates, the passengers walk down a long, futuristic tunnel with red carpeting. All in all, it's quite awesome.

That should do until one day you get to see it for yourselves.

Ta Ta –
Christine

April 20, 1964

Dear Folks

I'm hoping you had a happy 35th anniversary – did the flowers and present arrive on time? And, I trust you had a pleasant Easter – did you get the Easter lily I sent? I spent Easter Sunday in Paris - in bed, trying to thaw out a cold. If I were an American Indian, my name would have been "Running Nose."

Had my hair lightened a few shades last week, and now I can definitely verify the truth of the adage that blonds have more fun. At least, more fun than mousy browners.

Guess what – I have a new beau here in New York. His name is Gary – 27 – lives in the Village – has a car – and is really smart – sometimes sounds like he swallowed a dictionary. He has worked for TWA for about six weeks – in some department I can't remember the name of, but it's part of management – he works in the 605 Fifth Avenue office. He thinks I have great legs. Isn't that a gas? Once again, the game is afoot!

Are you planning to come here for the World's Fair? I understand it will be a mob scene in New York this summer, so if you're planning to come, might I suggest September or October? My roommate Katy said the other day that nothing in New York surprises her any more, except maybe finding a parking space.

Love, Love, Love –
Christine

April 20, 1964

Buenos Dias, Mary –

Latest news flash! I have a new love interest in Madrid – his name is Jeronimo (the J is pronounced like an H). He's about 6'2" with blond hair and quite a handsome face – in a patrician sort of way. When I first met him he spoke not word one of English, but his friend told me that after he met me he started studying English, and after about a month, he's now discussing philosophy in English! Ha ha. My attempts to speak to him in my pitiful Spanish evidently afford him some pain. My last trip he took me to a football game – Madrid was playing against Valencia – and J is from Valencia. Don't know who won – we got rained out. Their football is like soccer. They play with a round ball and hit it with their feet and heads and knees – everything but their hands. Seems very effortful.

I've decided that J could never be my soul mate, though. He's very reserved, and it's more than just shyness. Spanish men are very proud – with a great big P. When I'm with him on a sunny afternoon, and we're promenading in the Retiro (big park) and acting very dignified, I feel like I've gone back in time about 100 years. Then the next day I fly home to New York and the Swinging Sixties. My version of time travel.

Hasta Luego –
Chris

May 17, 1964

Hi, Mom and Dad –

I must hasten to tell you about one of the girls I'm flying with this month, who is a such a stitch. She has blond hair and a rather large battlefront (big boobs) and her name is Joan. (The purser is fond of singing "Joan is bustin' out all over." He continues to think it's hilarious no matter how many times he sings it.) Now, some people are of the opinion that Joan is not what you might call a serious thinker. She walked into the galley at one point during the trip and said, "A passenger just asked me if I had met Mr. Right yet. Doesn't he know the Wright brothers have been dead for years?" Later on she was telling me about an emergency on one of her flights where they had to make a "premature evacuation." And she told us about the paintings she had seen in London's National Gallery - of famous people who were "immobilized" in oil.

She calls the cockpit crew "the Holy Trinity" and calls pilots "egos with legs." The purser said to her, "You should have a little respect for the cockpit crew." She replied, "Oh, I do have – very little." When she takes coffee to the cockpit, she says to them, "May it please your worships….."

She's pretty easy to find – you just follow the trail of laughing passengers.

Love, Love, Love –
Christine

May 17, 1964

Hola, Mary –

I've been seeing Jeronimo for about six weeks now, and I've found out lots more about him. He has finished medical school and is a full-fledged neurosurgeon, but now he's on a scholarship studying Social Medicine (whatever that is – his English isn't the best, so I understand maybe every other word he speaks.) Anyhow, as you may know, Spanish people are pretty poor, but he's student poor, too, so we can't afford to do much. We mostly go to the Prado (art museum – free) or take long walks and sit at sidewalk cafes and drink one Fanta (soft drink) for about three hours and try to figure out what we're saying to each other. Last trip we went to the bullfights. (Ava Gardner was sitting across the stadium from us in the front row.) I bought the tickets at the hotel and pretended that a passenger gave them to me. Spanish people have a lot of pride, so you have to be careful.

But, this Saturday he took me dancing on the 25th floor of the best hotel in Madrid – glass all around with a beautiful view of the city, and we drank champagne! Don't know where he came up with the $ for that, but we'll probably be back at the sidewalk cafes from now on. He's kind of shy and not forthcoming with compliments, but this time he said he likes me because I'm tall and have blue eyes (his are brown). Then later, after swilling more champagne, he said he loves me. (At least, I think that's what he said – he pronounced it "lups,")

Hasta Luego –.
Chris

June 26, 1964

Dear Mother and Daddy –

I love, love, love Switzerland! I'm flying to Zurich this month, and it is the cleanest, neatest place I have ever seen. On every block there are beautiful gardens with gorgeous flowers.

We stay in Wintertur, which is a small town about 20 minutes out of Zurich on the train. The only drawback is that Switzerland is evidently the most expensive country in Europe. This is the only place we fly to that, instead of giving us per diem for expenses, the company pays for all meals we have at the hotel – we just sign for them. Which is nice if you plan to spend the layover in the hotel, but what fun is that, I ask you?

Last trip we took the train to Basel and saw the point where France, Germany and Switzerland meet. (I didn't even know they did.) It was a beautiful day, so we had a lovely view of all three countries. We plan to take the train to Lucerne next trip to see Wagner's home.

Gotta flee –
Christine

June 26, 1964

Hi, Mary –

Did you get my post card from Aruba? I went there by myself because neither of my roommates got the time off, and I had a whole week between trips. My round trip fare was only $10, and I had a beautiful double room overlooking the swimming pool and the ocean for $8.50 a night (regularly $17). It's a tiny island – part of the Dutch West Indies – right off the coast of Venezuela. The people speak Papiamento, which is a blend of English, Dutch, and Portuguese.

There are lots of little trees there, called Divi Divi trees, which look like they're all blowing one way – even when it isn't windy – because of the trade winds. The sand is really white, the water crystal clear and calm. (Is this beginning to sound like a vacation brochure?) The sun, however can be brutal. I spent a day in it, the result of which was a weird mixture of tan and burn on my outer crust.

I made the mistake of having dinner the first night with a fat guy I met on the plane, for lack of anyone better to have it with, so the next day everywhere I went, there he was – in the hallway – in the lobby – at the pool, swooping down on me, insinuating himself into my personal space. I didn't encourage him – he just adhered. I had trouble curbing the impulse to tell him to "Bugger off, so I can meet someone else!"

Later –
Chris
P.S. Got a nice letter from Jeronimo, who is back in Valencia for the summer. He wants me to come back to Madrid, but I've already bid Milan for next month.

July 21, 1964

Hi, Folks –

This month I'm flying to Milan – with three flying partners who seem to be just as frantic as I am to see everything we can possibly see in the world. Our first trip there, we got up early and took the train to Venice, where we had an idyllic day. (Did you get my post card?) It was the most beautiful weather in the history of the world – we rode down the Grand Canal in a gondola and fed the pigeons in the Piazza San Marco – and ate at a sidewalk café - just like in the movies. It was a great experience - the only drawback was that it entailed a four-hour train ride each way. We had to take the slow train – none of us being willing, or able, to afford the fast one.

Meanwhile, back in New York (is this sounding more and more like a movie?) I recently met an Englishman under fortuitous circumstances (we were eating at the same lunch counter), and we've subsequently been out a couple of times. One of the things I love about him is his name – it's Alastair Sebastian Cavendish. Isn't that just too, too aristocratic? And, I love his Englishisms. When he asked me out, he said, "I'd rawther like to see you on Friday night." When we stopped for gas, he said it was necessary to "call for petrol." And when we went to order drinks, he said, "A scotch and splash would not come amiss." And to me he asked, "Will you have something moist?"

What a gas!

Ciao –
Christine

July 21, 1964

Dear Mary –

I'm flying Milan this month, and it turns out that Milan is a great city to go other places from. (Or, as a more literate person would say "from which to go to other places.") My first side trip, along with three other hostesses was to Venice, which couldn't possibly have been a more delightful experience. However, we didn't fare as well on our second venture.

Our plan was to take a train which we thought would deliver us to Florence so that we could spend the day gawking at astounding works of art. When we first got on the train, we walked back several cars to find four seats together, ending up in the rear section of the train (our fatal error), which subsequently disconnected from the front part of the train in Bologna, and instead delivered us to Rimini, a beach town on the opposite (east) coast. So, we spent the day at the beach, trying to figure out where we went wrong. The moral of the story being that travel is fraught with peril, so one needs to remain ever vigilant. My flying partner says that we weren't lost so much as "investigating alternative destinations."

I have since bought a Berlitz Italian phrase book for travelers – an edifying work of literature.

Ciao –
Chris

August 4, 1964

Hi, Mother and Daddy –

Had a super layover in Milan last week – three of us took a train to Genoa – saw Christopher Columbus' house – then we went to Santa Margerita, Portofino, and San Fruttuoso – all on the Italian Riviera. That day we took 2 trains, 3 busses, 1 taxi and 3 boats, and I saw the most beautiful scenery I've ever seen. There are mountains all along the coast, and the water is a dark turquoise blue – just gorgeous.

Back in New York, I'm having great fun with my dear, sweet Alistair. One day we took the Hydrofoil boat to the World's Fair – went to about a dozen of the pavilions – had dinner at a Spanish restaurant – got home about midnight. The next night we had Italian food (not at the fair) – the next night Chinese food – and the next night American food. Then the following day we rented a car and drove to Jones Beach. Alistair had bought me a little portable chess set to play with at the beach, which we did, and I promptly beat him three games. He calls losing, "a spot of bother."

New York is great in August – everyone is somewhere else.

Love, Love, Love –
Christine

August 27, 1964

Dear Mary –

Pour yourself a libation and settle back while I tell you about
-The Brian Affair:

Part I: Brian lives in Chicago. He's a small, compact,
bursting-at-the- seams-with-energy kind of guy – very cute
and charming and lots of fun. I met him through a friend of
a friend. I see him whenever he comes to New York.

Part II: Last week Brian came to town – we went to see
Barbra Streisand in **Funny Girl**, and that night he gave me a
big, showy (ugly) ring from Tiffany's that he had once used
as an engagement ring for a former fiancee, who married
someone else and lives not far from me here in New York
City.

Part III: Last night we double dated with said former fiancee
and husband – went to Basin Street East to see Mort Sahl
and Nina Simone (my absolute fav singer of all time). But,
as the evening wore on, Brian and FF became more and
more engrossed in each other, laughing and flirting and
ignoring everyone else around them – leaving me miserable
and mortified. So, along about midnight I excused myself,
got up and walked out the door, got in a cab, and came home.
And, I hope never to see him again in this life or the next.

Epilogue: I mailed him the (ugly) ring.

Ciao –
Chris

September 23, 1964

Hi, Folks –

I'm so excited! You know how you've been wanting me to get you a painting from Paris, Mom? Well, I'm flying with my roommate Lori this month, and our last trip there we went up to Montmartre, which is an area where artists sit outside around a big square and paint and sell their work. One of the artists had a style that I loved a lot, and I would have bought the very painting he was working on, but of course it would have taken a long time to finish and then to dry. So, the artist took us up to his garret, which was nearby, to see the rest of his work – plus his wife and *bebe*. I wish you had been with us – his little studio is way up in an attic and looks like it was right out of a movie set. And, the three of them looked like they came straight from central casting.

I know you are going to love the painting I chose for you. Instead of having you pay me for it, I would like to give it to you for Christmas. Think you can wait that long?

That evening we went to the opera and saw **La Boheme**, and, *voila*! The stage setting looked exacty like the artist's studio we had just been in!

Love, Love, Love –
Christine
P.S. Hope you had a happy birthday, Mom, and that the flowers and present arrived on time.

September 23, 1964

Hi, Mary −

News Bulletin. My big sister Ann just produced yet another offspring − and it is yet another boy − their fourth! Their names are Kenny, Kevin, Kelly, and the latest addition, Kurt. Guess I'll have to weigh in with a present for the new one at some point, which I can't wait to do, because it affords me the chance to go to the baby store and look at the cutesy little stuff. I fervently wish they would succeed in spawning a girl for a change (I'm sure they do, too) − so I could go shopping for some cute baby girly things.

Which reminds me − I recently had a little American boy on flight who had made friends with a little Italian boy who was sitting near him. So, just before the movie came on, the little American boy came up to me with his movie headset in his hand and said, "Do you have any of these in Italian?"
　　Isn't that sweet?

Ciao −
Chris

October 8, 1964

Dear Mother and Daddy –

I've been sitting here searching for the right word to describe my latest trip (debacle springs to mind). Actually, it was more like a series of shocks. It was an impromptu trip for which I was – shall we say – ill-prepared.

My regular schedule had me going to Paris on Wednesday of this week. So, Monday morning at 9:00 A.M. Crew Scheduling called (I was still abed, needless to say) and informed me that they were short of girls and that I had to check in for a Washington DC – Frankfurt flight in three hours! At this point it was all I could do to overcome my first impulse, which was to hang up and rip the phone cord out of the wall. But, instead I told him – truthfully – that my uniform (jacket, both skirts, coat – everything) happened to be in the cleaners, but unfortunately my plight met with an unsympathetic ear. He informed me that I would just have to work the flight without a uniform! At first I thought he was joking! Who ever heard of such a thing? That's the stuff nightmares are made of.

I considered this to be an emergency of sorts and proceeded accordingly, i.e., I (1.) pushed the panic button (screech!), and (2.) called the hostess office all in a dither and was told that they had some uniform items there in the office that I could use. So, I grabbed my crew kit, hailed a taxi and hightailed it out to the hangar. After trying on exactly 1,000,000 skirts, I found one that fit, but they had no jackets or trench coats, so I had to go jacketless and wear a winter coat. I actually made the noon check in, totally frazzled. And that's when the fun began.

Turned out we were delayed several hours out of New York – got into D.C. late – went out to dinner with the crew and then saw the movie **Becket,** which I loved. The next morning I trudged all around town – in the rain – trying to find some place that would put those little lifts back on my heels – with no luck. That evening we (I, liftless) went out to the airport at 6:30 P.M. for the Frankfurt flight, only to be told that the airplane was still in Halifax, where it had to stop for fuel, and that it would be in around 10:30. After we sat around for a few hours, they cancelled the flight, and we went back to town and spent another night in D.C. The next day we worked the flight to Frankfurt, and all was routine, except that we had to make an unscheduled stop in London and change airplanes. When I finally got to my hotel room in Frankfurt, safe from all the slings and arrows of outrageous fortune, it was so cold I slept in my slip, nightgown, slipper sox, winter coat and two fat comforters. Seems they don't turn the heat on in that hotel until November.

Coming home the next day our departure was delayed three hours for a fuel leak. I was saying to myself that nothing could surprise me now, and then something did. When we got to New York, the air traffic was so heavy we had to land in Boston and fuel up in order to come back to New York and circle two hours before we landed. I overheard my flying partner telling a passenger that we would be landing at JFK any day now.

As I keep telling you, this is SUCH a glamorous job!

Love, Love, Love –
Christine

October 28, 1964

Oh, Mary –

Absolutely THE MOST WONDERFUL thing has happened!!!
I'm in love again!! Let me go into reverse and fill you in.

Do you remember Jason, the guy I told you about
who lives across the hall and has beaucoup bucks and is *tres
distingue* and took me out once a year ago and never called
back? Well, every now and then I run into him in the hall or
on the elevator, and we exchange a few pleasantries. Friday
late afternoon I ran into him again, and ten minutes later
he called and asked if I would like to come over for a drink,
which I, of course, hastened to do. So, we had a couple of
gin and tonics, and he asked if I would like to go out to
dinner, which we did, and I enjoyed it immensely. He went
home to New Jersey, where his parents live, for the rest of
the weekend, and I flew on Sunday, so he said he would call
me on Tuesday night when I got back. That was last night,
and sure enough he called and asked me over for a drink,
and then whilst we were drinking he asked me out to dinner
again. After dinner we went back to his apartment and talked
until 1:00 A.M. He's extremely easy to talk to – very witty
and very, very nice. (Did I mention that he is a Leslie Howard
look alike?) When he walked me to the door last night he
gave me a quick kiss on the lips. Isn't that sweet? I think the
Jasons of this world are on the verge of extinction. He just
called me tonight and asked me to a movie tomorrow night –
I'm all a twitter! He's a good Catholic, so nothing will ever
come of it, but meanwhile, he's entirely irresistible.

Ciao –
Chris

October 28,1964

Hi, Folks –

I've had a couple of trips to London this month. The theater there is really cheap and easy to get tickets to, so last trip I went to see **Oliver** – can you believe I sat in the front row of the balcony, and it cost me only one pound (about $2.40)? Then on another trip I went to a play with a Hindu fortune teller I met on flight. He looked at my palm and told me that I'll be married by 1966, that I will have children, and that my husband will be very happy with me. Also, he said that 1971 will be a very good year for me financially. (But, what am I to do in the meantime? You may well ask.)

I love London – the English couldn't be nicer or more polite, and – guess what – they speak English! Kinda fun for a change. And they have pubs! Which are very fun! In the pub one can have a Shandy, which is beer and lemonade, and which is surprisingly tasty.

I'm flying with Joan again this month – my blond friend with the large frontal lobes and the wry sense of humor. On one flight I noticed a male passenger showing off his muscles to her, and I overheard her say, "The length and breadth of the British Isles will be quaking in their boots when they see you." She refers to suitcases in the overhead rack as "carrion luggage." And, of one very obese passenger she said his stomach boarded the plane about 5 minutes before he did. And, when a passenger asked her to bring him a cup of coffee, she said, "I'd like to, but I'm having labor pains." She tells me she drives a Ford Pudenda.

At one point in the flight a few of us were sitting in the galley talking about pets, and one of the girls was telling us about how she had just had to have her dog put down and how devastating it was. So Joan said, "Yes, I had to have my husband put down. It was heartbreaking."

Ta Ta –
Chris

November 29, 1964

Dear Folks

I fear my luck is showing a distinct downward trend. A couple of weeks ago I got a letter from my old paramour Jeronimo (who is teaching Neurology in Valencia now) saying he was going to be in Madrid the same day as I was (we've kept in touch, so he knew my schedule). Of course, I wrote back telling him how delighted I would be to see him again.

So, the day of the trip I set out for the airport – left the same time I always do – but I couldn't get a cab to the East Side Terminal because the traffic was unbelievably heavy – I've never seen it that bad. I finally talked an off-duty cabby into taking me, but by the time I got there I had missed the 4:00 bus to JFK, so I took the 4:15 bus, which would have been okay, except the driver didn't know which route to take (somebody forgot to write it down for him), so we got all entangled in the traffic. As a result I checked in 25 minutes late, and they had taken me off the trip and called a reserve. Now, normally if this happens and you can catch the reserve before she signs in and tell her that you really want the trip, then if she's nice enough, she'll let you have it. (This is what I'm told – I've never been late before.) So, luckily, I caught the girl on the stairs as she came in, and I explained the situation – about keeping the tryst with J – and she replied, "Well, I've never been to Madrid before – I'd rawther like to go." (English girl) I, lower lip trembling, pleaded with her with all the eloquence I could muster, but she just shrugged her shoulders and walked away.

It taxed my self-control to the utmost to refrain from giving her a karate chop to the windpipe. Instead, like any red-blooded American girl, I burst into tears and went home to Midtown Manor and ate a whole quart of butter pecan ice cream.

Love, Love, Love –
Christine

November 29, 1964

Hi, Mary –

My last trip I worked First Class with a very sweet little hostess who had just started flying – she working the aisle and I the galley. At one point she was going around pouring hot tea from a silver pot, and as she was leaning over to pour tea into 2A's cup, there was a little jolt of turbulence, which resulted in the hot tea landing just short of his cup and onto his knee. She was so horrified, she exclaimed, "Oh! I'm SO sorry I tord hot pee on you!" Hahaha

The Jason Saga continues: We did go to the movies the night after I last wrote – then for drinks. We had sort of an average time, and he gave me another quick kiss on the lips and said "maybe" he'd call me next week. I wasn't counting on it, but he did call after all, and we went out to dinner and had the best time ever. He said he'd call me on Sunday. He didn't. But he did call on Monday, and we went to the movies again. I had dirty hair and looked sort of scuzzy, so we had only a mediocre time. I wasn't even rewarded with the usual smack on the lips when we parted.

But! The following Thursday we were having drinks and dinner, and after a few Scotches, he got all talky and complimentary – he said I have nice hands – that he loves the way I talk – and that I'm a thinking person. (Oh, be still my heart!)

I walked around for a couple of days, thinking, "Isn't life just one grand sweet song?"

Love –
Chris

December 8, 1964

Hi, Folks –

Just got back from Madrid again –it was actually a routine trip – hallelujah! On the way home we had the mayor of New Orleans on board and also a funny comedian who told me that our food is so good he wished he had two stomachs. On deplaning, he offered to give me a lock of his hair. Also, there was a little fat boy on flight who came back to the galley and asked me what we were having for dinner. When I told him it would be chicken, he shouted, "CHICKEN! I LOVE CHICKEN!!!" When I laughed at him, he got all serious and told me that he would "try to make room in his schedule" for dinner.

Looks pretty likely that I will be able to come home for Christmas this year. I'm trading into a flight that will get me back to New York on the 21st, so I'll be home on the 22nd, but must leave Christmas morning to be back to work a trip to Rome on Christmas night. I will have to leave your house at 10:10 A.M. on a flight that connects to a 1:30 flight out of O'Hare – landing in New York at 4:20, in time to check in at 6:45 for my trip. That is, providing my trade goes through. I fervently hope it does. Fingers and toes crossed.

Wouldn't it be nice if I could just put on some sparkling red shoes, click my heels together three times and say, "Home" (or whatever it was that Dorothy said), and I would be home?

Love, Love, Love –
Christine

December 8, 1964

Yo, Mary –

Latest Jason Saga update: I came in from a Madrid flight on Tuesday night and had just walked in the door and, lo and behold, the phone rang, and, another lo and behold, it was our boy Jason. So, we went out to dinner at an Italian restaurant, but I was SO tired that after only two drinks I was sort of – you might say – catatonic. At the end of the evening I got an unexpected smack on the lips, but I was too pooped to pucker.

Wednesday night I was a first-nighter! Alistair and I went to the opening of a Broadway play called ***Poor Richard*** – then out to dinner at an Indian restaurant and then dancing.

With the holiday looming over our heads, Katy and I went Christmas shopping Thursday night, along with 99% of New York City, all of them wild-eyed with consumer panic – and then we had dinner at P.J. Moriarty's. It was her last night in New York before moving to London to get married. She'll be working for TWA in Reservations over there. She's such a dear friend, and I will miss her inordinately.

I've had two offers for New Year's Eve, but I really wish Jason would ask me – I adore him.

Gotta dash –
Chris

December 18, 1964

Hi, Folks —

Had a super layover in Madrid this week. The evening we got there the whole crew met in the hotel bar for drinks and then out to dinner. As we were finishing our Paella (a dish made of garlic with a little rice and meat thrown in), a group of young Spanish college guys came around our table and played guitars and sang to us. Their enthusiasm was so infectious that we followed them to a bar, where we bought them Sangria (a sort of a fruity wine punch), and they sang to us some more, and then they sat with us, and we entertained them with 14 of the 15 words we knew collectively in Spanish. After that we went to a place called The Cave and drank more Sangria and inflicted more of our fractured Spanish on some more Spaniards – then went with them to a club to see flamenco dancing. We got back to the hotel at 4:00 A.M., and I slept like a baby.

By the way, what's with that expression? Don't babies wake up and cry all night?

See you soon –
Love, Love, Love –
Christine
P.S. I just read a quote by Groucho Marx. It goes, "Believe me, you have to get up early if you want to get out of bed."

December 18, 1964

Hey, Mary –

More of the Jason Saga: Ran into Himself in the hall on Monday night, and he asked me over for a drink. (Sounds like we've gotten into a rut, huh?) He had to go to a dinner that night, and I had a blind date, but he said that he planned to be home early, and if I was too, he'd call me and we could get together and do something. Well, it turned out I didn't get home until late, so I don't know if he called or not. (I'll bet that about now you are thinking I've become obsessed with this guy, but that's really not true. I can actually go several minutes at a time without thinking about him at all.)

The blind date that night was fun – I fixed up a girl I'd flown with and we doubled – went drinking at the Four Seasons. (Another celeb sighting – Bob Hope was there having dinner.) The next night I went to a party and dinner with dear Alistair.

The following night Jason called me to go out to dinner, but I had a date, so he asked me for the following Monday night – the first time he's ever asked me in advance. Maybe now he'll begin to see that I'm not always at his beck and call. Actually, I am, but he doesn't need to know that.

I bid you a Merry C and a Happy N Y –
Love, Chris

January 7, 1965

Dear Mom and Dad –

After leaving your house on Christmas morning, I met with a series of minor ups and downs. (Yes, dear readers, it's another of those yay/boo letters.)

No doubt you'll be happy to hear that luck was with me getting back to New York that day. I made the earlier flight out of O'Hare (yay), although my suitcase wasn't so lucky (boo). I actually had a couple of hours in Midtown Manor before heading back out to the airport to work the flight to Rome, and fortunately, my suitcase had turned up in the interim (yay).

We were a few hours late leaving for Rome (boo), but we had only a smattering of passengers (yay), so I got to read uninterrupted for most of the flight. It was pouring rain in Rome the whole layover, and nothing was open (December 26 is treated just like December 25 there - boo), so we all hibernated for the day. The next morning we worked a flight to Paris, and that night, in spite of the fact that it was bitter cold and snowing, we went to the opera and saw *Faust* and then had pizza (yay).

The next day on the way to the airport our crew bus broke down (boo), so we had to sit there and shiver for an hour until another bus came for us. Then our airplane was late coming in, so our departure was delayed a while (boo), but we had only a handful of passengers on board, so I got to watch the movie *Topkapi* with no intrusions from the inmates (yay).

Thanx for all the great gifts – their abundance bespeaks generous hearts. Sooooooooo good to see you both again. Have a First Rate New year.

Love, Love, Love –
Christine

January 7, 1965

Hi, Mary –

How was your New Year's Eve? Mine was just okay. Alistair had a party at his apartment, and then we all went to the Scarsdale Country Club and drank champagne and danced. I got numerous compliments on my dress – a pink brocade affair with long sleeves. However, all the guys wore tuxedos, and I was shocked to the core to find that I was one of only four ladies there who was wearing a short skirt! Naturally, when I danced – reluctantly – it seemed to me that everyone in the room was frowning at my all-too-visible legs! I felt like my legs were blushing.

On New Year's Day Jason called and asked me over to watch the Rose Bowl game with him, and of course, I fell all over myself getting across the hall post haste. We drank lots of beer while I feigned enthusiasm for the game – and then we went out to dinner.

Have I mentioned that I've been wanting to live in an apartment on my own at some point? With that in mind, I've been tramping around the upper east side every day, looking at various and sundry (mostly loathsome) places. One of them already had an occupant – in the form of a cockroach so enormous that I'm sure it is the envy of the animal kingdom.

Ciao –
Chris

January 21, 1965

Hi, Folks –

Just got back from Rome – that's where I'll be flying this month and next – out on Sunday and back on Wednesday. It's a non-stop with two days in Rome, so I feel pretty lucky to be able to hold it. This last layover we went to the opera and saw **The Marriage of Figaro**, and the next day we went to the Vatican and saw St. Peters and the Sistine Chapel. That night we went to the opera again and saw **Tristan and Isolde**. This was the first Wagner opera I've been to. I've always wanted to see a Wagner opera, but now want to see all of them.

My flying partner gave me a great tip about how to resuscitate one's feet after hours of slogging up and down the aisle on the airplane. It goes like this: Sit on the edge of the bathtub – run hot water over your feet – as hot as you can stand it for a few minutes. Then do the same with cold water, and keep alternating that way for a while. Your feet will be miraculously rejuvenated – enough to take you dancing all night.

Love, Love, Love –
Christine
P. S. A former navy pilot told me this joke: Know the definition of a formation of Navy planes? Two planes flying in the same direction on the same day.

January 21, 1965

Hi, Mary –

Latest in the Jason Saga: I went over to his apartment and watched TV with Himself one night last week and ditto the week before, then out to dinner after – nothing new there. We seem to be stuck in the quick-kiss-on-the-lips-on-parting stage of what might loosely be called - our relationship.

Guess I told you I've been wanting to find a place to live alone – an idea I've not entirely abandoned - but apparently Fate has decreed otherwise. I've decided to move in with two hostesses, one of whom is a very sweet girl I've been flying with. They have a pretty cool place on 57th Street, which is a wide street with a plethora of nice shops and art galleries. They have a doorman, maid service once a week, a telephone answering service, and once-a-month window washing. And, my share of the rent will be only $86 a month, because it's unfurnished – the furniture belongs to one of my (future) roommates. Also, my name won't be on the lease, so I can move whenever I get itchy feet.

And, best of all, it's only three blocks from our present apartment building, which is where Jason lives. We'll soon see if he thinks I'm worth a three-block walk.

Ciao – Chris

P.S. Have you ever smoked marijuana? Well, one of my roommate's friends brought some over to our apartment the other night, and we gave it a try. After a few puffs, for some reason every time we began a sentence, we would get about half-way through and then totally forget what we were talking about. So, it was one of those evenings where we thought we had a lot to say, but nothing much ever really got said. But, what actually did, seemed to us for some reason to be incredibly funny.

February 20, 1965

Hi, Folks –

This is shaping up to be a memorable month. Besides having a birthday (yay) and the flu (boo), I moved into my new apartment, which turned out to be a major effort – and also spent a few days in San Francisco helping my old roommates, Dyan and Judy, move to their new apartment.

Here's how that came about: Susanne was in New York on a layover, and she talked me into using a pass to fly back to SFO with her and stay in her new studio apartment. She got a place by herself so she can practice her (rented) piano without disturbing anyone. So, after an emotional reunion with D and J, I was promptly put to work carrying a hundredweight of their belongings down three flights of stairs from the old apartment and up one flight to the new one. My legs are still sore. We had nice weather to do it in, though. Apparently it had rained 36 days in a row before I got there!

My move in New York was not exactly a stroll in the park, either. Two of the guys I'm dating have cars, so they each helped me with a load – I didn't want to impose on them more than that, so I ended up making seven walking trips myself. Thank goodness it's only three blocks (yay), but it was bitter cold and windy (boo). It was well worth it, though. The girl who owns the furniture (Bunny) is sort of an amateur interior decorator, so the apartment is *tres* elegant – all light and white and modern. We've named it Tajma Hall.

Love, Love, Love –
Christine

February 20, 1965

Bonjour, Mary –

Last week I traded into a Paris trip. It was supposed to be only a 17-hour layover – out Tuesday morning – home Wednesday night – but the flight we were to take home originated in Rome, and it was cancelled because of the big snowstorm there. It was the worst snowstorm in Rome since 1796! Good thing I traded out of that flight, or I would have been right there in the thick of it. Although, on the other hand, it would have been a novel experience.

Are you up for another episode of the Jason Saga? Hope so, cuz here goes: Himself didn't call for three weeks (!) after I moved. I was beginning to sense a lack of interest when, just in time to snatch me from the jaws of despair, the phone rang, and (be still my heart) it was HE! I had to break a date to go out with him, but of course that's a minor prob. He came over (actually walked the three blocks – yay!) and met my new roommates – he seemed impressed with Tajma Hall (name of the new apartment) – then we went out to dinner.

The next week he called and asked me over – turned out to be the night before he left on vacation, and I was pretty excited that he wanted to spend it with me (the evening – not the vacation). Upon parting, full of love and vodka tonics, I moistened my lips in the highly unlikely event that he would give me a long, passionate kiss, but I got only the predictable smack on the lips. Disappointing, but exciting, nevertheless.

Adieu,
Chris

March 31, 1965

Dear Mom and Daddy –

Must tell you about the new man in my life – we've dated for a whole two weeks now. His name is Patrick, and (he says) he used to be a famous folk singer, but he is now P.R. Director for **Household Magazine**. The only drawbacks are that he is 43 and has been married three times, but he is very sweet and kind and, of course, dripping with charm.

New, as you know, hope continues to spring eternal, so with that in mind, I took to the kitchen once again the other night with the object being to cook dinner for Ye Olde Patrick and me. This time I tried to make French fries (cut my finger while slicing the potatoes – washed the blood off my finger, then washed the blood off the potatoes), but the oil burned over – then I burned the garlic bread, and then I burned my finger on the coffee pot. There it was again – another humiliating descent into the depths of incompetence.

My roommate says that in the kitchen I'm a "menace to man and beast." Apparently, I have nothing to bring to the kitchen but a compelling appetite.

Patrick hasn't called me back. Perhaps he's moved on to an alternate food source.

Love, Love, Love
Christine

March 31, 1965

Dear Mary –

No Jason Saga this month – neither he nor Patrick (new man – older – Rock-of-Gibralter type – father figure) has called lately, so last night I went out with a Pan Am pilot, who took me to see **The Odd Couple,** which is a new hit comedy on Broadway, with Art Carney. I cried. But, it was from laughing so hard.

A couple of weeks ago I went to a small party in Patrick's apartment, and at one point we happened to hear a woman singing – in a beautiful operatic voice. P said, "Oh, that's probably Maria Callas – her voice coach lives in this building." I was thrilled.

I'm flying to Rome again this month, and on my last trip I overheard one passenger in First Class telling another passenger that when she takes a night flight to Europe, like the one we were on, her "circadian periodicity gets all fucked up." Ha!

Ciao –
Chris

April 23, 1965

Buenos Dias, Madre y Padre

As you may have guessed, I'm flying to Madrid this month – the weather there is really lovely this time of year. The climate – and the countryside – remind me a lot of California. My last trip the whole crew went to the roast-suckling-pig restaurant I told you about, (which I am told, by the way, is the oldest restaurant in the world) where we ate in an unbridled fashion, leaving only devastation behind. They're not on the menu, but if you know enough to ask for them, for dessert they serve tiny little wild strawberries – with fresh whipped cream – that are very rare and very sweet. Words have not been invented to describe how delicious they are.

Also, I'm having a jazzy dress made there – a baby blue silk, sleeveless, A-line, double-breasted affair. Which will work out perfectly for my double-breasted body.

Just got back from having two of the shots (cholera and smallpox) that the company gives us periodically, and they've made me sooooo sleepy. I think I'll go and (as they say in England) "have a little lie-down."

Adios –
Christine

April 23, 1965

Hi, Mary –

Continuation of the Jason Saga: After two months of deafening silence – to the point that I thought he had blipped off the screen – I had a message from the answering service when I got in from flight Wednesday night that HE had called! He left his number, and I didn't know if that meant I was supposed to call him or what. So, I didn't. Then Thursday, just as I was leaving, he called and asked me if I was happy now that's it's warm (70 degrees that day), and of course I was ecstatic, but not because of the weather. So, he said he would call next week, which met with my hearty approval. Whenever I talk to him – either in person or on the phone – I always feel like I've just swallowed a whole flock of butterflies.

Just found out my roommate Bunny is moving to New Jersey and, of course, taking all the furniture, so I'll be moving yet again. Annie (other roommate) and I want to get a place together, so because I have five days off and she has six, and because our passes came through on time, we're going to the Virgin Islands in order to have a good long talk about it – and maybe get some sun and do some sightseeing, too. We're going to St. Thomas, St. John, and St. Croix (pronounced CROY).

Romance and adventure beckon!

Ciao –
Chris

May 27, 1965

Hi, Mom and Dad –

In answer to your last letter, Mom, yes, I did have my Illinois driver's license renewed through the mail. They also sent me a Certificate of Commendation from the state for not having any violations in the last two years. Seems I've discovered the perfect way to maintain a spotless driving record – by not driving at all.

Since we're soon losing a roommate (and her furniture), Annie and I have now decided WHEN to move (July 1), but we've yet to determine WHERE. We've done some apartment hunting, and there seems to be plenty of places available, but nothing approximating what we can afford to pay.

Did you get my post card from St. Croix? We went there for two days and then on to St. Thomas. We were there for the carnival and, in order to enjoy it to the fullest, I called up and went off schedule so I could stay another three days. My excuse was that I had an awful sunburn, which I subsequently did.

We have new summer uniforms this year – they're not exactly what you might call *haute couture*, in fact they're downright ghastly – blue skirt, white jacket with blue flecks, and a blouseslip of a different blue with a tab hanging down from the collar, embroidered with a cheap-looking TWA emblem on it. The hat looks like a mushroom sprouting from my head. I don't know what to do with the hat, but if I had to make a list, "apply to top of head" would be dead last.

The whole get-up is totally dorky.

Love, Love, Love –
Christine

May 27, 1965

Hi, Mary –

I'm having a perfectly splendid week: Monday night Patrick met me at the airport with a big kiss and a box of candy – then out to dinner. Tuesday night I went with Alistair to see *Flora, the Red Menace*, a Broadway play starring Judy Garland's daughter. Then last night I went out with the Pan Am pilot again, and tonight Jason (!) and I are going to dinner and a movie - *Mirage*, with Gregory Peck.

More of the Jason Saga: More? You are probably asking – doesn't anything new ever happen with these two? The answer is a resounding NO. Or, YES, depending on how you look at it. You might compare it to a snail chasing a turtle.

The first week of the month we went out two nights in a row – the first night he actually said he missed me! The second night we saw *Zorba the Greek*. Don't know if I'm making any headway with him, but at least I'm keeping him in my crosshairs. Still the same tender little lip smacking at the end of each date. Which, believe it or not, I really look forward to.

Ciao for now –
Chris

June 24, 1965

Dear Folks –

I read the other day that Manhattan Island is 22.7 square miles in area, so what would you think the chances are that I would be at Your Father's Moustache (jazz place in the Village) on my way to the loo, at the exact same moment (two weeks ago today at 10:00 P.M.) as Ralph, the person I'm now engaged to? That's how it began, by my giving him my phone number, his calling the next day, our going out that night, his proposing to me, my thinking he was kidding. The following day he took Annie and me to the airport, and when I got to the hotel in Madrid there was a telegram waiting for me with another proposal. When I got home, he was waiting at the airport (he was driving a black Jaguar XKE, which is my dream car, but it turned out to belong to a friend of his). The next day he helped move Annie and me into our new apartment.

The night we called you, we were at the Playboy Club with Annie and Ralph's roommate. It was Ralph's idea to call you, although we couldn't hear much of what you said because of the general din. The next day he bought me The Most Beautiful Ring. It's made like a flower with Florentine gold leaves and a diamond in the middle.

I'm not rushing into anything just yet, but Ralph is SO much fun to be with – great personal magnetism, laughs a lot, talks to everyone, is interested in everything, always there with the witty repartee. He reminds me of the description of Teddy Roosevelt - that he was like "a steam engine in trousers."

As you know, I've had a couple of proposals before, but I've never actually been engaged. It's kind of fun! And, I love the ring!

Love, Love, Love,
Christine

June 24, 1965

Hi, Mary –

End of Jason Saga (he hasn't called for three weeks). Beginning of Ralph Saga: I met said Ralph two weeks ago – got engaged (!) a few days later. He is 6' 3" – 33 – blond – wears glasses – nice looking, with a bigger-than-life personality. When he introduced himself, he said his first name was Alias. He's SO much fun to be with – has sort of a sweep-you-off-your-feet way about him so that you just kind of go along for the ride and hang on for dear life! (Was that three clichés in one sentence? Guess I'll never get a Pulitzer Prize.)

I'm well aware that a bit of caution should be exercised here. But on the other hand, when I get old, I want to be able to look back on my reckless youth with the confidence that it was sufficiently reckless.

Watch this space for further developments.

Adios –
Chris
P.S. The other night he said to a bartender, "I'll have too much to drink, please."

July 23, 1965

Dear Mother and Daddy –

I would like to go on record as stating that I yield to no one in my hearty approval of long engagements. Mine, however, did not fall into that category. I'm no longer in possession of the pretty ring. My affianced turned out to be mostly talk and little else – altogether an inferior grade of human being. He has a way of thinking of the truth as being only one of life's possibilities. His motto seems to be, "Who needs the truth if it's dull." Now that I've seceded from the union, I must admit that I was temporarily snowed by his smooth-talking big city ways. I had to wait for my brain to gain momentum in order to see my error in failing to notice all the little clues that pointed to the fact that he may not be an honest, upstanding citizen. End of subject.

    I'm flying to Merry Olde England tomorrow, and I'm really looking forward to seeing Katy. Did I tell you she's pregnant? Yes, folks, another dear friend has fallen into The Baby Trap! There seems to me to be widespread reproductive activity of late, no?

    Also, it looks as though Annie and I are coming to a parting of the ways. As you know, we had decided to furnish an apartment together, but it turns out that we have wildly different tastes. For instance, she wants us to have a red couch and black-and-white print chairs (!). Also, it promises to be more than I wish to afford. I think the $ would be better spent on an exotic vacation or two. So, it looks like I'll soon be resuming my favorite hobby – apartment hunting.

Love, Love, Love –
Christine

July 23, 1965

Dear Mary –

End of Ralph Saga: Suffice it to say that when the scales fell from my eyes, I found him to be altogether irresponsible and untrustworthy (also jealous and possessive). Back to the Jason Saga: Went out with The Adored One the other night and had a perfectly lovely time. He said he has spent only three nights in the city in the last two months – the rest of the time at home in New Jersey. Apparently his mother is dying of breast cancer.

My vacation is going to be in November this year – not that I bid November, but that's all I could hold, since I'm so junior on International. When Susanne was in town recently, we got together and (over several gin gimlets) found that, since we both have an overwhelming curiosity about the USSR (Russia), why not go there and experience first-hand that famous Russian winter? I've read a lot of their fascinating history, so it's been a long term plan of mine to see all their famous places, like the Hermitage, Red Square, the Gum Department Store, Catherine's Palace, and Lenin's Tomb. They have preserved his body so that you can actually see him.

Adventure beckons!

Love,
Chris
P.S. Remember Joan, my dumb-like-a-fox flying partner with the ample bosom? Well, we were working First Class together the other day when a passenger asked for more caviar. As I passed by pouring wine, I overheard her expressing her amazement that he hadn't yet heard of the Great Caviar Famine of 1965.

August 18, 1965

Dear Folks –

Today Annie and I signed the papers releasing our apartment for sub-letting, and they informed us that we have to be out by the 18th of September. So, starting tomorrow I'll be back out there pounding the pavement in search of new digs. (Seems like we've heard this once or twice before, you're probably saying to yourselves.) As you know, I'm no stranger to apartment hunting, but this time I'll be looking to be snugly housed in a studio for one - not counting the odd cockroach or two.

Did I tell you that Susanne and I are planning to go to the USSR on our vacation in November? We have been advised that before we can get a visa, everything (hotel, transportation, etc.) must be prepaid, and all the arrangements have to be made through Intourist, which is their state travel agency. So, while we will be restricted in what we can see and do there, it will be an easy trip in the sense that we will be taken care of at almost every step by an Intourist guide.

I've had a couple of trips to London since I last wrote. On one flight we had Cary Grant and his new wife in first class. They had just gotten married, and he was taking her to England to meet his mum. On the other trip, I had a good long layover, so I saw Katy, who is living there now, and saw two plays and bought a new dress. I was wondering why the dress was so short, until I was told that it is a mini-skirt. Apparently they are really "in" now.

Love, Love, Love –
Christine

August 18, 1965

Greetings, Mary –

Jason Saga: not much to report – The Object of Desire asked me out once recently, but I was nursing a pretty intense hangover (the revenge of the demon rum), and my hair looked dreadful, so I had to regretfully decline.

I've been seeing Ralph again now and then. He professes to be an actor. He is also a writer, depending on to whom he is lying at the time. He says he threw the ring in the East River the night I gave it back. Don't think I'll be seeing too much more of him – it's too tedious. I've come to the conclusion that I temporarily took leave of my senses and delivered myself over into the clutches of an authentic sociopath! With a lifelong preference for fantasy over reality.

Last week I had a few days off, so I used a pass to go to San Francisco to see the SFO faction – that being Susanne. We saw a couple of movies and did our usual all-night blab-fests, and while I was enjoying myself, it crossed my mind to move back there, but the next day when we stepped outside and were being blown thither and yon by the blustery wind, I nixed that idea. Also, as you've probably gathered, the dating scene is 1,000 % better in New York.

Ta Ta –
Chris

September 20, 1965

Hi, Folks –

Have you ever felt like you wanted to simply press a button and disappear into the ether? I just got back from a trip to Madrid, where I was afforded the opportunity of proving once again that there are endless ways of embarrassing oneself. Here's one way: When we got to our layover hotel, the Castellana Hilton, there were no clean rooms available for us, and we were told to wait nearby until they were ready. So, I sat down on a couch in the lobby, and after being up all night to get there, I promptly fell into a deep, relaxing sleep. When I woke up several hours later (my hat on the floor and possibly some slobber on my chin), there was a stringed quartet playing nearby, and people were sitting all around me having drinks. Nobody seemed to notice me (or were polite enough not to seem to) as I slunk off to my room with as much dignity as the circumstances permitted.

Celebrity sighting! Remember the last time you came to New York to see me, Mom, and we saw the play *A Funny Thing Happened on the Way to the Forum*? Well, in Madrid I saw Zero Mostel, who was the lead in that play, in the chi chi men's shop at the hotel buying some classy duds. He's so cute!

Glad to hear you liked the watch I got you for your birthday, Mom. I got it in Zurich last spring and have been worried all this time that you wouldn't like it. I had thought of throwing sanity to the winds and trying to sneak it in through Customs, but in the end I decided to declare it and pay the duty, because I felt that you would probably prefer to receive my letters from New York rather than from behind bars somewhere.

Love, Love, Love –
Christine

September 20, 1965

Hi, Mary –

Did you know that the U.S. has military bases in southern Spain? Me, neither. I just got back from working a military charter – taking troops to Madrid. It was a balance trip (which means that if Scheduling determines that you haven't flown enough hours for the quarter, they stick you on an extra trip).

We (crew) left from the hangar at JFK on the Air Taxi Service to shuttle over to McGuire Air Force Base in New Jersey, where the flight was to leave from. These shuttles are small planes that hold only 5 people, plus the pilot. Well, evidently the gods were angry that day. What should have been a fun little flight turned out to be, for lack of a better term, a dead scary experience – in the form of a thunderstorm that we thought we were on the edge of, but it turned out that we flew right through the middle of. The whole flight the rain was pounding on us, there was lightening all around us, we were bouncing all over the place, and we were all scared to death! The pilot was trying to look casual, as if flying head-on into a thunderstorm was something he does every day. He almost landed at two different little airports before we got there (about 100 years later). Amazingly enough, we all came through the ordeal with dry underwear.

On that layover we all went on a tour to the north of Madrid and saw the Valley of the Fallen with a monument to all the soldiers who died in the Spanish Revolution. Also saw the summer palace of the old kings of Spain. Then we went shopping at the Rastro, which is a huge flea market, rife with scads of things you can afford but don't want.

No romance to report – I'm too busy apartment hunting.

Hasta Luego –
Chris

October 23, 1965

Dear Mums and Daddy –

News Flash! No more pounding the pavement – I found an apartment! It's on East 73rd Street – a sublet for one year and three months for $130 a month. It's a fourth floor walk-up – has just one room, plus separate teeny kitchen, bathroom, and two closets. The single window commands an unobstructed view - of a brick wall. But it's mine! Since it's located uptown, I've named it Upton Downs. I'm moving in November 1 – also packing for vacation that day and then leaving for Moscow on November 2.

Doesn't look like I'll have a chance to come home before Christmas this year. I'm flying 86 hours this month (that's a lot, in case you didn't know – anything over 70 hours a month is overtime). What with vacation, moving, Christmas shopping – also the various TWA activities they dream up to take up our time off – like uniform fittings, the annual emergency review, yearly physical, innoculations, etc., I'll be under full steam for the next couple of months.

I have to bid for next year's vacation before November 1, and I get my two free passes to Europe after March 25. Do you want to use them? Apprise me.

Adventure beckons!

Love, Love, Love –
Christine

October 23, 1965

Hola, Mary –

Susanne was in town on a layover this week, so we spent the day at the World's Fair. The fair is closing soon, so the various pavilions are selling off their contents – the Israeli Pavilion is even selling fur coats. We talked non-stop about our upcoming trip to the USSR. Intourist has assured us that the visas are in the mail, so all we have to do is make airplane reservations and dig out our warmest duds, and November 2 we're off to the races. I bought a Berlitz phrase book in Russian, and I'm learning the Cyrillic alphabet, which is not much like ours at all. Susanne says we are "trembling on the edge of life's next adventure."

Did I tell you we'll be there for the big annual celebration of the winning of the October Revolution? They celebrate on November 7 because they were on a different calendar back then. So, we'll be in Moscow until the 11th and then, clad in thermal underwear, we will take a train to Leningrad and see if we have the strength to withstand the famous Russian Winter. My roommate cautions that we should examine our hotel rooms to see if they're bugged. As far as I'm concerned, I'll be happy as long as we have indoor plumbing and aren't literally bugged – with real bugs.

I have only one more trip before we leave. My schedule has been grueling this month. I've been flying to Rome - the flight doesn't leave until 10:00 P.M., it's an 8-hour flight, always chockablock, and we've had supervisors on three out of four flights so far this month. Also, we go out every six days, which gives us only three days at home at a time. The only positive is that I will be acquiring vast sums of $ in overtime. Huzzah!

Ciao –
Chris

November 21, 1965

Hi, Folks –

Our trip to the USSR was THE MOST FASCINATING
EXPERIENCE that Susanne and I have ever had or are ever
likely to have. Here's how it went:

We took SAS to Copenhagen - spent a day there
sightseeing and shopping – then on to Helsinki overnight.
The next day we took Aeroflot to Moscow. By the time we
got settled in our hotel, the National, which is very historic,
apparently, it was late afternoon, so we walked across the
street to Red Square, which was sooooo exciting! There were
spotlights and posters everywhere and soldiers practicing
marching for the big annual parade on Sunday – to celebrate
the winning of the revolution.

The next day our guide took us on a tour of the city in
a car which appeared to be the only car in the whole city. At
one point we briefly saw another car in the distance, but that
was it, traffic wise. We couldn't wait to get to Gum – their
big department store. The building is enormous - takes up
a whole block. It's just gorgeous, with rooms for dozens and
dozens of shops, but the shops were totally empty except
for one, which was a "Beriozka" store, or what they call the
"dollar store," because they accept only American dollars,
which Russians aren't allowed to have, so the shop was almost
empty of customers. There was very little for sale, and what
they had was expensive and of poor quality – NOT what you
would call a shopper's paradise. The next day we went inside
a cathedral in the Kremlin where all the czars were buried
up until the 18th century – and then into the Armory, which
is a museum displaying the clothes, jewels, Faberge eggs,
carriages, uniforms, armor, etc. belonging to the czars. That

night we saw *The Barber of Seville* at the Bolshoi Theater. Tickets were only five rubles (about $5).

Sunday we watched the big parade from what had to be the best vantage point in the whole city – our hotel room. We were on the fourth floor in a corner room with a balcony overlooking Red Square. We could see the parade coming from all three directions and converging right under our window – then going on into Red Square. There were lots of big tanks and missiles and what seemed like hundreds of troops. Then, toward the end, two soldiers with rifles came into our room and stood on our balcony, while a convertible drove all around the intersection, with guess who standing up in it and waving – Kosygin and Breshnev! It was soooo thrilling!

The next night we went to the new Palace of Congresses in the Kremlin, which is a gorgeous modern building made of marble. We saw a political opera called *October* – all about the revolution, obviously. (It was pretty ho hum.) Next day we went to Tolstoy's house, where our guide pointed out a stuffed bear in the house, which she said had "barely" killed Tolstoy (she meant "almost"). Then that evening we went to a dacha in a village outside of Moscow.

Thursday night we took a train to Leningrad, which is about 500 miles north – it was dark almost the whole way, so we couldn't see anything out of the windows. It was very comfortable, but it took six hours to get there. It was bitterly cold in Leningrad – even in our hotel room. The next day our guide took us on a tour of the city, and that night we saw *Swan Lake* at the Kirov – on the same stage and by the same company (different people, of course) where it premiered in 1877. Next day we spent in the Hermitage – stayed until closing time. The following day I went there again, but apparently there was an exhibition of French paintings on loan from the Louvre, so I was presented with a looooong, unmoving line just to get inside that curled all around the building, which is about the size of Montana. I waited over an hour until I couldn't feel my feet anymore and then went back to the hotel and crawled into bed to thaw out. We found out later that it was the coldest November 15 in Leningrad's history!

Going home we took Aeroflot to Helsinki. It was a rickety old plane with no seatbelts and luggage piled everywhere. There were actually people who didn't have seats standing in the aisle the whole flight! And, while we were taxiing out to the runway in Leningrad, looking out the window we could see hundreds and hundreds of airplanes parked in rows – that you couldn't see from the terminal. We spent a few hours in Helsinki and then took SAS to Stockholm and spent a day there. There were no concerts or operas that night, so we went to a Beatles movie called **Help** (spelled "**Hjelp**" in Swedish).

We didn't buy much – I bought a balalaika, an amber necklace, a picture book of the USSR, and some things for you guys which I will save until Christmas.

Das Vidanya –
Christine

November 22, 1965

Dear Comrade Mary –

Despite the sense of never quite knowing what was going on, we had a terrific trip to the USSR! The people are such a kick! The first night we got to Moscow we walked across the street from our hotel to Red Square, and we started talking to two students named Michael and Sasha. Sacha spoke no English, but Michael made up for him and did the translating. They were as wildly curious about us as we were about them. Michael is without a doubt the funniest character I've ever met. He is a small, dark, wiry guy, who looked a lot like Lenin, but with hair. He talked incessantly, asked us tons of questions, and made jokes and then laughed at them. He tried to talk politics with me – in vain, of course, because I have no clue about world affairs. For instance, he asked me if I wondered why they invaded Yugoslavia (I didn't even know they did), and he proceeded to tell me all about it in an unending stream of fractured English. Sacha was a tall blonde with a baby face.

Every time we came out of our hotel, there they were. At one point they insisted on coming up to our hotel room, and when the concierge (there's one on every floor) yelled at them and tried to keep them out, Michael yelled right back and called her a "fats piggy." (She did, in fact, run to surplus poundage.) Michael went straight into our bathroom and stayed a long time, and when Sacha finally went in, there was Michael in the bathtub having a bath.

One night they took us to a party – just a few young people – in a girl's apartment where she lived with her family in 3 rooms with a kitchen they shared with another family. Their custom seems to be that you never drink by yourself; you wait until someone makes a toast and then you all drink together, downing everything in your glass (vodka) like we used to chug-a-lug beer in college. Their vodka isn't as strong as what we're used to, but after (in the spirit of bonhomie and good will) we toasted each other and each other's countries numerous times, the hostess got sick and threw up all over.

Another night we went with them on a train to Sacha's father's dacha in a woods of birch trees outside of Moscow. It was all dark and spooky, except for a little store that looked like a frontier outpost right out of a movie of the Yukon – a log cabin with only one candle for light, meat hanging down from the ceiling, and lots of shelves with not much on them. There was one little old man working there - all bundled up, since there seemed to be no discernable heat. Michael bought some cognac, because that was all they had in the way of spirits.

When we got to the dacha, Sacha realized he had no key, so he broke a window, climbed in through same, opened the door, and invited us into an eerie room, remarkably devoid of any light, heat, or furniture. So, lest we seem ungrateful, we sat ourselves down on the floor and shared the cognac, mentally smiting our brows and having trouble resisting the impulse to run like the wind.

At the end of the week we said our *das vidanyes* to them and took the train to Leningrad. The next morning we were having breakfast in the hotel lobby café, and who should walk in but you guessed it – Michael and Sacha! I think all Russians are kind of crazy. They should never ever have been let in on the invention of liquor. They eat and drink and smoke – all at the same time. It seemed to us that most of the populace was perpetually drunk (maybe to stay warm?). But – eccentric as they are – you can't help liking them.

Das Vidarya –
Comrade Chris
P.S. No bugs of either kind in evidence.

December 28, 1965

Dear Hearts –

What great news about Ann's new baby – and Keaton is such a neat name! Do you think they'll keep trying for that girl – or call it a day after five boys? Tell me if I have their names right – there is Kenny (8), Kevin (5), Kelly (3), Kurt (1) and now Keaton (0). They've spawned their own basketball team – and they will literally own the team. I will be weighing in with a present for babycakes forthwith and posthaste. Speaking of basketball, Susanne's current boyfriend plays for Cincinnati, so when they played in New York a couple of weeks ago, she got us free tickets to the game. Too, too exciting!

News Flash! I should like to announce that instead of your heretofore having had one old-maid daughter, you now have an old-maid daughter who has flown one million miles! I was awarded my million-mile pin last week.

I'll be spending New Year's Eve in Madrid this year – probably in bed with an edifying work of literature. But, it is worth it to have had Christmas off to spend with you. I had a perfectly splendid time whilst at home – thanx for everything!

Love, Love, Love –
Christine
P.S. Quotation from Groucho Marx: "Outside of a dog, a book is man's best friend. Inside of a dog, it's too dark to read."

December 28, 1965

Dear Mary –

Guess what. My sister Ann just had her 5th baby boy! Lordy, lordy. Hope you had a good Christmas – I got to spend it at home with my parents this year.

Had kind of an exciting scare recently flying from Milan to Rome. We landed in Rome, stayed down for about five seconds and then took off again! Apparently, the doors that open to let the landing gear down weren't locked in place, so we had to prepare for an emergency landing, but then we ultimately landed without incident. As we were taxiing to the gate the passengers were "making a joyful noise unto the Lord."

The trip I'm flying this month is a real killer. Coming home from Madrid we stop in Lisbon, Santa Maria (Azores), Boston, and then New York. So, from the time I leave the hotel in Madrid until I get home to Upton Downs it takes 16 hours. The first time I did it, I came home and slept 17 hours the first night and 12 hours the second. I think a steady diet of that trip would cause one to age faster than one year per annum.

Now that I'm in a whiny mode, I mustn't neglect to tell you about my missing crew kit, which was lost on my last trip before I went home for Christmas. As a result, I had to buy all new stuff to replace what was in it, including the presents I had bought for my parents. Then just yesterday they found it, so I didn't even get reimbursed, except for the travel alarm and transistor radio that were missing. And my parents each got double presents for Christmas.

I flew with funny Joan again recently. She said she thought she should have gone into a more suitable line of work – like stomping grapes.

Happy New Year –
Chris

January 10, 1966

Happy New Year, Mother and Daddy—

I just got the funniest letter from one of the Russian students who glommed onto us in the USSR. His name is Michael, and he's really a character. So, I just have to pass along some parts of the letter to you—the parts I can make out.

"Let me congratulate you, your friends and your parents with Christmas and New Year. Who was born to creep can't fly. Today is Saturday now is evening and I make up one's mind write for you. The time go pass very slow and agonizing. I am quarrel with Sacha because don't like his double game. He is not my real friend more. He called you old pepper-box. Beloved Chris! Why did you are so cruel to me? Why you are so cool? Why you don't believe me? Let us analyse meeting of us. Let us be impartial"......"Do you think I am against Mr. Kennedy? Do you think I am for Hitler? No, I do not. Why is it can be so? I am friendly to everybody, but not everybody friendly to me"........ "Write me please if you want and if it is not against of your individualism. What exchange in me do you want to see in the next ten years? Get up to famous?"..................... "Write me you believe that I don't want powder of your brains"........... "Let us be out spoken. Did you said you individual want do thinks and love with people who you love but not with who love you? Individual from good people, but you want to have good clothes? What for? For looks good? For Frank Sinatra? For people who get up very high or to people which you know too mush?"

And, it rambles on and on for ten baffling pages.

Love, Love, Love—
Comrade Christine

January 10, 1966

Hi, Comrade Mary—

Here is an excerpt from a ten-page letter from Michael, the student I told you about in the USSR.

"I tell you why I was wrote all of this because real friends must be frankly. I talk about real strong friendship. Mistake of me was made when I forget about prejudice, but you no. Did you compare love and like to politic. Do you think that intelegence now can be only in U.S.?"........ "Let me wish you happiness and lucky in the sequence year. Read more Russian writer Chekov".......... "Excuse me that I can't give you my true address where you can write me constantly. It is very canger to write about politics or affairs in the letters, because many of them open's in the boarder for secret police for look how and what for write to anywhere. So, please not write me about it in your letters." (Then he gives me an address.) "Not have mistakes in the letters. Address you write in such order. It is writing on the post office and not in my address because after travelling me nowhere to leave."

You know, I shouldn't really make fun of him—he's writing not only in another language but also in another alphabet. I can't imagine even trying to do that.

Das Vidanya—
Comrade Chris
P.S. I just found out that lots of famous people have stayed in the National Hotel where we stayed—for instance H. G. Wells, Prokofiev, Pablo Neruda, Van Cliburn, John Steinbeck—and lots more.

February 18, 1966

Hi, Mom and Dad—

I've been flying like mad lately. Week before last our Madrid flight cancelled, so they sent me on a long trip to Paris and Rome. Then last week I had two days in Madrid after only one day at home—then two days off and a trip to Paris, Milan, and Rome. The night of my birthday I flew to Rome—we got about two hours out over the ocean when one of the engines stopped, so we had to land in Gander and wait there until they fixed it. We were so late getting into Rome that by that time we had been up all night, all day, and well into the next night. I've had better birthdays. All of them, to be exact.

As I may have told you, there has been an extended strike of NYC bus and subway employees, and it actually impacts everyone who tries (in vain) to get a taxi, and of course, the problem is compounded during the rush hour. One week, in order to get to the East Side Terminal and thence to the airport, I shared a cab with four other people— it took one hour and 45 minutes to go 30 blocks, but only cost me $3. The taxi driver was bragging that his cab could go from 0 to 5 MPH in 20 minutes. The next week I shared a cab with another lady—that took an hour, and I had to walk 12 blocks. I'm thinking of investing in a pair of roller skates.

Just another sampling of the glamorous life of an airline hostess.

Love, Love, Love—
Christine

February 18, 1966

Oh, Mary—

Congratulations on writing a book!! And getting it published!!
I am so proud of you! And not a little in awe of you! And,
not a little envious, too. To be an author would be my dream
come true. Let me know when it comes out—I want to be the
first (of millions) to buy a copy. And to tell everyone I meet
that I knew you before your name became a household word!

Have you read *And Quiet Flows the Don* by Mikhail
Sholokov? I just finished it and loved it. Everybody in Russia
(that is, the 4 people we met who spoke some English) was
talking about the author - he won the Nobel Prize last year.
It's about the Cossacks during WW I and the Bolshevik
Revolution. It's kind of like *War and Peace*, only a century
later, and it's about poor people instead of rich ones.

Ever so many thanx for the clever birthday card. Ralph
gave me a big fat dictionary, of which I was in dire need.
My old one dated back to the Truman administration and
had been my constant companion during and since college.
Speaking of constant companions, Ralph continues to adhere,
with no encouragement. He seems to think marriage might
improve him. It's difficult to imagine anything that wouldn't.

Gotta flee—
Love, Chris

March 20, 1966

Dear Mother and Daddy—

Had an excellent trip last week—a day in Paris, a day in Milan and a day in Rome. In Paris I finally went up in the Eiffel Tower (after three years of flying there). In Milan I went to La Scala and saw the ballet **Cinderella,** and in Rome I finally got to linger at the Trevi Fountain without having to contend with all the summer tourists flocking around it. Remember the movie **Three Coins in the Fountain**? That's the one. Yes, I did toss a lira into the fountain—seemed sort of mean spirited not to, in spite of the fact that I will undoubtedly be back to Rome countless times.

At the beginning of the month I enjoyed an unexpected eight days off. Apparently I was too high on time for the quarter (our union contract says we can fly only 235 hours in three months), so Scheduling took me off my first trip. I hadn't put in for any passes to go anywhere, so I spent the time in a violent frenzy of spring cleaning my new apartment. I believe I can state without fear of contradiction that Upton Downs has never ever been so clean—it positively reeks of Turtle Wax, Comet, and Mr. Clean. Also of Raid because I've been doing battle with several battalions of ants in—of all places—the bathtub. I think I'm victorious. I suspect I flushed about 1,000,000 dead ant bodies down the commode. Ignominious way to die, huh?

Tha-tha-tha-tha-that's all folks—
Love, Love, Love—
Christine

March 20, 1966

Yo, Mary—

Had my hair cut this week here in New York. The hairdresser who cut it has one of those dreadful East Coast accents. He informed me that, "Ya heeya—it's like buttah." I think he meant that my hair has no integrity, and he's quite right. However, I treated the comment with the silent contempt it deserved.

I ran into my weird ex-roommate Ronnie at the airport the other day. I made sure to not speak to her first, before she could have the opportunity to not speak to me.

Jason Saga Revisited: Finally went out with The Adored One again last week. We had dinner at a Jamaican restaurant. We mostly talked about furniture—seems he is furnishing an apartment, too. But, easily the high spot of the evening was when he said he had missed me! My joy was unbounded.

Love,
Chris
P.S. If no news is good news, this letter is full of good news, huh?

May 1, 1966

Hi, Mother and Daddy—

Mayday! Mayday! No, nothing is wrong—it's just that I can never resist saying that on May 1.

I'm off schedule now. Just spent a couple of days in the hospital having a lump removed from my breast. It was benign—no probs. I know what a worry wart you are, Mom, so I waited until it was over to tell you. Old Faithful Ralph took me to and from the hospital and surprised me with candy and flowers. I came home from the hospital yesterday, and the doc said I would be tired for a while, but - *au contraire* - I just finished vacuuming, washing and waxing my minuscule kitchen floor, fixing dinner, doing the dishes, having a bath and washing my hair—and I feel fine. Guess I inherited my bounce-back ability (resiliency?) from you two—thanx 1,000,000!

I flew to Rome in April—full loads with only three days off between flights (we call that 3 on, 3 off)—Rome again this month with four days between flights (called 3 on, 4 off) and six days off at the end of the month (I call that very lucky). I may go to Acapulco with my new friend Bridget if I can scrounge up any $ - after paying the IRS $200. I made the vast sum of $7,000 last year, so of course, I'm expected to share.

Love, Love, Love—
Christine

May 1, 1966

Hi, Mary—

Had a fun interlude recently—Susanne was in town for three days with her new (rich) boyfriend, so the four of us (me with Ralph) went to Dawson's Pub, which is one of my favorite places, then to a disco and then to a cocktail lounge on top of some tall building—I forget which one. Did we have fun you may ask? Well, yes and no. Suzanne and I had a splendid time, but I don't think the guys had such a good time. I suspect they were jealous of one another. They kept verbally sparring with each other the whole evening—in sort of snappish tones. The next afternoon Suz and I saw the play **On a Clear Day You Can See Forever** and then had cheesecake at Lindy's—just like tourists.

My funny friend Joan was on my last flight. She said she had been chatting with a passenger who told her his travel insurance covered falling out of an airplane, but not hitting the ground. Later in the flight, I overheard a lady passenger say to her, "You'll never believe this, but…" And Joan promptly said, "No, I don't believe I ever will."

On that same trip we had a delightful comedian in First Class. When I went around taking names, I said to him, "Can I have your name?" He said, "You could, but I doubt it." He told me his best friend was very unlucky—he got mugged while trying to rob a convenience store. And, after every funny line he would yell, "ba da boom!" (Like a drum, you know.) Then when the flight landed and he was deplaning, he said to me, "I'll always cherish our time together. Ba da boom!"

Ciao—
Chris

June 15, 1966

Buenos Dias, Mom and Daddy—

If you're ever looking for a perfect place to vacation, Acapulco would rank right up there with the best. It's a gorgeous area with warm, balmy breezes, lots of sunshine, nice people and plenty of activities. (That sounded pretty good, huh? Do you think I should be writing travel brochures for a living instead of being trapped in a metal tube hurtling through space with masses of clamoring thrill seekers? Maybe.)

Bridget turned out to be a great travel partner on our trip to Acapulco. We did all kinds of fun things, including watching the famous cliff divers plummet into the ocean. They have to time it just right with the tide and the incoming waves to avoid being smashed against the rocks. Too exciting! Also, we went water skiing, and then we tried something new—Scuba diving. We took lessons in the hotel pool and then went down about 40 feet in the ocean to an old sunken ship. It was an interesting experience, but I don't think I'll ever want to do it again—its cold down there!

Faith and begorrah - I'm flying to Ireland this month. We fly into Shannon and stay in the little village of Limerick, which is beautifully lush and green. The Irish say there are "forty shades of green." (Actually, the way they say it sounds like "farty" shades of green.) The Irish language is sort of puzzling—I walked by a mailbox that was labeled "oifig an phoist." We were happy to find that the Irish people seem to genuinely like Americans. Also, the Shannon airport is a great place to go broke saving money.

However, you mustn't believe everything I say from now on, cuz I kissed the Blarney Stone whilst there.

Love, Love, Love—
Christine

June 15, 1966

Hi, Mary—

Did I tell you about my new friend Bridget? She and I just went to Acapulco together. She has a rich boyfriend who lives there—he owns a jewelry store. So one night they fixed me up with a friend of his, and the four of us went out together. The friend was good looking and apparently a rich jeweler too, but he turned out to be something very closely resembling a jerk— with all the charm of a Black Plague epidemic. Most of the evening he held us spellbound with his account of his recent bunion surgery—not exactly riveting. He was definitely not the Latin Lover we have come to expect.

One day B and I were sitting at a bar on the beach, and we struck up a conversation with some local guys, who wanted us to get in their car and go with them to a party at another beach. My instincts told me not to go, although they seemed really nice, and fun, too. So, we declined. Guess what—the very next day we read in the paper that a girl's body washed up on shore that morning—in that very same area. As Bridget so often says, "Danger lurks around every corner!"

Jason Saga: I've had no problem spurning his overtures— because he hasn't made any.

Hasta Luego—
Chris

July 10, 1966

Hi, Mums and Daddy—

Wouldn't you know it, just as the Carey bus workers went back to work after a 2-month strike, making it easier for us to get to work, now we're not working at all because our mechanics went out on strike. When it happened, I immediately called Kelly Girls, but alas—they have no jobs. Then I went to the Unemployment Office and found out that we don't get any compensation from them until the strike has been going on for 49 weeks! I can't afford to do anything, so I'm just sitting tight, trying to enjoy a vacation I don't need. Or want. To paraphrase Oscar Wilde, I'm wedded to poverty, but in my case the marriage is not a success.

Before the strike I had a trip to London, and I really got lucky—for some reason I got one of the best rooms in the hotel. I had a gorgeous view out of the window, overlooking Kensington Palace, where Margaret and Tony live. The desk clerk told me that Olivia Newton-John had just checked out of that room. I was flying with Lori, so we got together with our old roommate Katy, who (whom?) you remember lives there now, and we got to see her new baby girl. They can't afford a crib, so the baby sleeps in the top drawer of their dresser. Her husband babysat one night while the three of us went out to a play, and the next night she had us over for dinner. Also, we went to the Tower of London and saw the Crown Jewels, some prison rooms, and the place where Ann Boleyn was beheaded, which had kind of a sobering effect on us.

If the strike is over by next month, I'll be flying to Athens! Yay!

Love, Love, Love—
Christine

July 10, 1966

Hi, Mary—

A friend of mine who lives in a New York apartment says she considers a day wasted that doesn't contain the murdering of one or more cockroaches. Last week I killed three of the loathsome things in my apartment. One was so big it was possibly carnivorous. And one was actually crawling up my LEG! Eeew!! My first inclination, which is my response to every emergency, was to scream and run away. Where do they come from? They were all three in the bathroom. Do they live in the walls? Are they a family? I'm thinking maybe I should just sublet to them and move somewhere else. I've sprayed really well, so I'll be sleeping alone tonight—I hope.

Our mechanics are on strike now, and we are honoring it, so I have lots of time to do things but, unless something fortuitous should happen, I have no $ to do them with. I could look for another job in the interim, I suppose, but I see no reason why I shouldn't save my energy, which I am bound to need later in life.

Ralph and I have been to the beach a few times, and this week he took me to the Museum of Natural History (whoopee). The museum was more crowded than I've ever seen it—no big surprise, considering I've hardly ever seen it.

Its dinner time now, and I'm sitting here completely surrounded by no food. I'm not used to such Spartan fare.

Ta Ta—
Chris
P.S. I think it was Coco Chanel who said, "The best things in life are free—the second best are very expensive."

August 19, 1966

Hi, Folks—

What luck! I just flew two trips! In spite of the mechanics' strike, TWA is still flying the military charters (I guess they don't involve our mechanics), so apparently Crew Scheduling goes right down the hostess seniority list (there are about 1,000 of us on International) and gives the trips to whomever they can reach on the telephone. Fortunately, I was one of those whomevers, so I got to deadhead to SFO and then fly troops—on their way to Viet Nam—as far as Honolulu, where another crew took over. The boys seem so young— like teenagers. One of them came up to me and said, "What time do we get to Vanilla?" (He meant Manila.)

My other trip was to Madrid for four days. I'm just happy to have any trip at all—to ensure me those three squares I've come to depend on. Although, as soon as we get back from these trips, they take us off the payroll again. I'm amassing so many bills that when I get thrown out on the street for non-payment of rent, I can build myself a little house out of them.

The other night Ralph and I went to a N.Y. Philharmonic concert in Central Park—along with 75,000 other people. They played "Eroica," which is one of my favorites, and Stravinski's "Rite of Spring," which Ralph is wild about. The conductor was Leonard Bernstein, who we happened to see at the movies the night before. (The movie was **The Russians Are Coming**, which is hilarious—Alan Arkin does a perfect Russian accent.)

Love, Love, Love—
Christine

August 19, 1966

Aloha, Mary—

Have you ever tried to surf? I got to spend a few days in Honolulu recently on a military charter, so another girl and I threw sanity to the wind and took a surfboard lesson. I found it pretty easy to get up on the thing and to stay up for a while, but then each time after you fall off the board, you have to heave yourself back up onto it and paddle way back out there where the waves break, and it's utterly exhausting! Seems to me like a whole lot of effort for such a small thrill.

Last week Ralph and I went to an amusement park and had a fun day. Ralph yells at the top of his lungs on all the rides, even if they aren't scary, and it cracks me up. I was afraid to go on the big roller coaster, so we went on the kiddy rollercoaster instead. We were the only ones on it, so we sat right in the front—we could hardly fit in the little seats. The man running it really laughed at us cuz Ralph was yelling like he was scared to death.

I just finished reading **Catherine the Great** by Zoe Oldenbourg—it's fascinating. I had seen some of her dresses and carriages in the Kremlin Museum, so that made it all the more interesting. She led quite a life—had her husband killed so she could be the Empress and had a different lover every two years until she was about 50. Inspiring, don't you think?

Love,
Chris
P.S. I read a wonderful quote from Oscar Wilde the other day. "Be yourself. Everyone else is already taken."

September 4, 1966

Dear Mums and Daddy—

The mechanics' strike lasted 43 days! It ended just after I last wrote (whew—I was just getting ready to join the bread line), so I got to work two trips to Athens before the end of last month and one to Shannon this month before I go on vacation.

Think I told you at some point that my vacation is this month, and I'm going to South America with two other girls. One is an English girl—lovely person and very adventuresome. The other one is all bubbly and fun-loving, so since it's rumored that three heads are better than one, I think we're going to make an ideal troupe.

We're using I.D. 90s on a number of different airlines for the various flights (that means we pay 10% of the coach fare) and, of course, we fly standby, so as far as our schedule goes, we'll just be winging it (literally—ha ha). We're going to Lima, Peru first and hope to make it to Rio and Buenos Aires at some point.

If you don't hear from me in a couple of months, it will probably mean that we've met some handsome *caballeros* and decided to stay there and settle down.

Romance and adventure beckon!

Love, Love, Love—
Christine

September 4, 1966

Buenos Dias, Mary—

Well, in a few days I'm going to be "flying down to Rio," just like in the movie. Actually, we're planning to go to Lima, Peru, first and then over to Buenos Aires and then to Rio. My vacation is this month, and I'm going with two other hostesses that I really like. We'll be travelling standby, of course, so our itinerary will depend on the various airline flight schedules and open seats. (It won't be like in Russia, where we could just stand up the whole flight.)

To finance the trip I applied for a loan from the Credit Union, but when I checked in for my last flight, I was met with some disquieting news. Apparently I had filled out one of the loan application forms wrong. So, once again I'm encountering that deep gulf that lies between conception and realization. That's a long-winded way of saying I screwed up.

To quote Winston Churchill, "Success is going from failure to failure with enthusiasm."

Adios—
Chris

October 1, 1966

Dear Folks—

Got home from vacation yesterday - tired and broke. The trip was more interesting than it was fun. There were few facilities for tourists anywhere, and nobody spoke even a little English. South American Spanish is hard to understand, and in Brazil, where they speak Portuguese, we were totally baffled. One day in Rio we were on an elevator at our hotel, and when we reached our floor, I said to the operator, "Thank you," to which he replied, "Very much."

In Lima we really wanted to take a side trip to Machu Picchu, which is the mysterious ruin of an old Incan city on top of a high mountain, but Faucett Airlines (the only way to get there) just changed management, and they wouldn't give us a reduced rate, and we couldn't afford the full fare. That was a crushing disappointment. It was in Peru that I learned that drinking tap water is ill advised, even to brush your teeth. What's known as "La Turista" ensues.

Buenos Aires is a big European-type city, roughly twice as dirty as New York. We did some sightseeing (the balcony where Eva and Juan Peron made their speeches being the most memorable sight) then took the hydrofoil over to Montevideo—ostensibly for the day, but the boats were full coming back, so we spent the night there—sans suitcases. It turned out to be very fortuitous, though. We overheard some customers in a shop saying they were from the corps of the Kirov Ballet from Leningrad, and that they were performing there, so we went to see them that night. What luck, huh?

Love, Love, Love—
Christine

October 1, 1966

Buenos Dias, Mary—

Just got back from vacation—pretty interesting, but not all that much fun. We flew to Lima, sightsaw—then flew to Buenos Aires, sightsaw—and there partook of the *plat du jour*, which was tough beef (they apparently don't like their beef tender like we do)—then flew to Asuncion (capital of Paraguay) where we went to a place to hear what was supposed to be typically Paraguayan music. It was awful. Then we took a 10-hour bus ride to Iguazu Falls, which is on the border between Paraguay, Argentina, and Brazil, and which is now my favorite place on the whole earth. Definitely the highlight of the trip. We stayed at a hotel on a cliff overlooking the falls. They are pretty much indescribable—7 times as wide as Niagara and twice as high.

Then we flew to Rio (the Iguazu airport is just a little shed, and the runway is a field of grass), where it rained every day, so while we saw the famous beaches, we couldn't actually sit on them. It stopped raining the day we went up to Corcovado. Instead, it was so foggy we couldn't even see the top of Jesus' head. We expected some Divine intervention, but no luck—and thus no view. The next day we drove over to Brazilia, which is a collection of beautiful new modern clean white non-functioning buildings intended for the government - eventually. Divine intervention came after all in the form of gorgeous sunshine—just a few days late.

Love,
Chris

October 11, 1966

Dear Folks—

So nice to hear your voice on the phone, Mom, confirming that you and I will for sure be going to Europe together at the end of the month. I'll put in for the passes right away, so we can plan to leave on the 27th. I will bid lots of days off at the beginning of November, so we'll have 10 or 12 days over there. I get home from a flight on the 26th, but I'll have to stay at the airport for the ever-tedious Annual Emergency Training that night, which is supposed to last until midnight. Then I'll sashay home to Upton Downs, get a few hours' sleep, repack, and be ready to leave with you on the 27th. Damn the torpedoes! Full speed ahead!

Your pass to New York will cost $12 ($2 each way for service charge and $4 each way for first class surcharge). The overseas pass costs $48 ($18 each way for service charge and $12 for one first class surcharge), so it is $60 total. I figured out that if you were paying full fare for this trip, it would cost about $760. (Will that help to make up for all the grief I caused you growing up?)

Love, Love, Love—
Christine
P.S. Don't forget to get a smallpox vaccination, Mom.

October 11, 1966

Hi, Mary—

News Bulletin: I'm taking my mom to Paris and London for 10 or 12 days at the end of the month. As you know, she has scads of energy and such a great sense of humor that I think she'll be a kick to travel with.

Saw a cute play in London last week called **Come Spy With Me**. The best line in the play was when the girl was telling her boyfriend about a guy she had once gone out with, and he asked her, "Did you sleep with him?" and she smiled and said, "Not a wink."

Last night my old roommate Katy came over to see me (she + her husband + baby just moved back to New York from London). And, tonight Bridget—the girl I went to Acapulco with—came over for a while. Bridget wishes she were married and had a baby, and Katy wishes she were single and flying again. So, I guess I'm the only one who's happy with the way things are.

My other big news is that, after going out with Ralph for a year and a half, I finally broke it off with him for good. The uncoupling went pretty smoothly, but then a little while after he left, the doorbell rang, and it was a delivery of two dozen red roses from him with a card that read, ' I love you, Chris. Ciao." So, I had a good long cry—but no regrets.

Love,
Chris

November 9, 1966

Dear Mums and Daddy—

So glad to hear you got home okay, Mom, and that everything is tickety-boo, as they say in England. Are you regaling Daddy hourly with tales of our delightful exploits, so he'll be inspired to come with us next time? Hope so. I was so happy that we had nice sunny weather in London and doubly happy to find how nice everybody was to us in Paris—especially after I had cautioned you about how rude Parisians can be.

Did you hear they had snow in northern England after we left? And, speaking of cold, the boiler has been broken in my apartment building, so I spent most of Friday and Saturday in bed under my electric blanket that you gave me last Christmas. Had to boil water to wash my hair.

I'm flying what's known as a double crossing trip this month that goes from JFK to London, we lay over there a day, then London to Washington D.C., lay over a day there, then D.C. back to London, lay over a day there, then back to JFK. It's a 6-day trip, but I only have to do it twice a month. I'm on the D.C– London leg right now. Sure can't complain about the load. It's 0 in front and 21 in coach. The 21 inmates just finished doing battle with their chicken dinners and are now happily ensconced in movie watching. I think I'll join them. I read a quote by Alfred Hitchcock the other day—it goes: "The length of a film should be directly related to the endurance of the human bladder."

Love, Love, Love—
Christine

November 9, 1966

Greetings, Mary—

Well, I'm starting to get back in circulation again *apres* Ralph. Which is the natural order of things, don't you agree? Went out with a guy named Artie, who got my number from Annie. He's 36—divorced—extrovert—sales rep—played pro football until this season—races boats—good looking, in a studly football player sort of way, if you follow me. He seems interested, but I think he's too much of a party boy for me—doesn't read—doesn't like classical music. But anyhow, it's jump-started my move back into the dating circuit.

Flew with a girl my last trip who confided in me that she has "passenger relations" only with men who fly first class. Now, in my opinion, she can have all the affairs she wants, but I draw the line at talking about it.

Going from London to Washington D.C. yesterday a man from Africa was on the plane—all dressed in flowing robes and Arab headgear. He didn't speak English too well, apparently, because he came up to me and said, "Where is the lava? I want urinate!" So, after directing him to the "lava" and stifling a guffaw, I rushed back to the galley and told my flying partner. She said one of them came up to her once and said, "Where is the shithouse?"

Wouldn't you love to know what joker teaches them English?

Ta Ta—
Chris

November 28, 1966

Dear Folks—

Just got back from another unforgettable trip. Here are the harrowing details: We were scheduled to DHD (deadhead) to Chicago Friday night—work to London Saturday night and work home today. Well, Saturday night in Chicago the airplane for the flight to London came in from Los Angeles, but it couldn't land in Chicago because of fog, so it was diverted to Detroit. Our scheduled departure from Chicago was 6:30, so at 8:00 they sent us—with passengers—in smaller planes over to Detroit to meet up with the Mother ship, where we were further delayed, finally taking off at midnight. We had a full load of disgruntled passengers, and we weren't very gruntled ourselves.

Then last night in LHR I just could NOT sleep—floundered around in bed all night—finally got one hour of sleep (and woke up twice in that hour) and then worked the flight home today, but not without more tribulation. We were delayed getting into JFK because an Eastern plane had gone off the runway, so they closed that runway to clean it up. And, it was really cloudy and windy, so we had a pretty hairy landing. Then, I had to go over to the hostess office in the hanger for a uniform check, but I had to wait two hours for my supervisor because she was in another office. This put me on the Carey bus just in time for the 5:00 traffic tie-up, and it was pouring down rain in Manhattan, so I had to wait several years for a cab. By this time I had only a passing memory of what sleep is.

Such a glamorous job, huh?

Love, Love, Love—
Christine

November 28, 1966

Hi, Mary—

Did I tell you that TWA lost my suitcase the trip before last? It's still at large, and as a result I've had to replace a lot of belongings (makeup, etc.). So last trip I had to take all my stuff to the airport in a big brown shopping bag, get a new suitcase from the hostess office, and repack everything. On the way to the airport I told everyone who looked askance at my paper shopping bag that this was the new official TWA hostess suitcase—it's much lighter and has such easy access.

Did you have a nice Thanksgiving? I was planning to just have a peanut butter sandwich, but Ralph (yes, he surfaced again) called and insisted that I not be alone on Thanksgiving, so he came over to Upton Downs and cooked a 12-lb turkey and all the other traditional comestibles, all the while assuring me of what a good husband he would make. (I have no problem with him as a husband, as long as he is someone else's.)

I'm delighted to report that the dating pace is beginning to quicken. Tuesday night I went out with an Italian I met on flight. Wednesday Suzanne was in town on a layover, so we spent the day together, and that night I had dinner with Artie. Tonight, however, I've been home from London for 4 hours, and neither the Italian nor Artie has called. Frankly, my dear, I don't give a damn.

Ta Ta—
Chris

December 13, 1966

Dear Folks—

In the Good News Department, I got my first bid this month—I'll be flying the military charters to Saigon, with layovers in San Francisco, Honolulu (two days there each way) and Okinawa. So, it looks like I'll be in Honolulu for Christmas and San Francisco for New Years.

That bid has a lot of overtime, which I need, but I'm mainly looking forward to being in warm weather and basking in the Hawaiian sunshine. Also, I will be able to see my old roommates, Dyan and Judy, in SFO, whom I haven't seen in a couple of years. And, I can use my J Magnin charge card to buy Christmas presents and avoid paying for them until sometime in January. Brilliant, huh?

Ann sent me the Sears and J C Penny's catalogues to shop for the boys for Christmas, thinking that would save me some $, but if I do that, I wouldn't be able to go into FAO Schwartz and have the pleasure of playing with all the toys (and ultimately pay for the privilege).

Love, Love, Love—
Christine
P.S. I had a Russian passenger on flight recently who came up to me and said, "I am a Pepsi." I took that to mean that he wanted one. I was right.

December 13, 1966

Hi, Mary

Had a strange experience a couple of weeks ago. I found myself sleeping 12-14 hours every night, and having to lie down and fall asleep several times during the day. I was really baffled—what was causing my lassitude? Then on Friday I found out that it was due to air pollution in the city. Apparently a count of 12 is average for New York City, 50 is considered dangerous, and 60 is critical. Well, Thursday it reached a count of 80! Radio and TV broadcasts were asking people not to use their incinerators or drive their cars. It was all foggy out, and the city smelled like garbage. The next week the stagnant air began moving out, and it was back to normal (normal for New York City, of course). I'm told it might have been even worse if New Yorkers hadn't been out of town for the holidays.

On a lighter note, I flew with Joan recently—remember her? The funny one with the sizeable forefront? When I told her that a passenger had just asked me for some water "without gas," she said, "Well, that's up to him." Later, when one of the passengers on our flight asked her out, she told me she was "searching for words in which to make plain how little it appealed to me." When I asked her how she got out of it, she said, "I gave him your phone number." She obviously marches to the beat of an unusual drummer.

Still no sign of my suitcase.

Love,
Chris

January 6, 1967

Happy New Year, Mom and Dad—

So glad to hear you loved the ring I gave you for Christmas, Mom—I bought it in Rio. The stones in the ring are topaz, which is your birthstone, and are supposedly imbued with the power to dispel worry and bad dreams. So, wear it to bed, and let me know if it works.

Finally got home late last night—this trip was about as long as my vacation—15 days. We were supposed to be back the 1st, but the flight schedules got all fouled up due to a mechanical and some cancellations, so they sent us over to Saigon (from Okinawa) twice. We ended up spending Christmas in Honolulu and New Years in Okinawa. Actually, it was a really fun trip—I flew with a girl who used to date the same TWA captain that I did in San Francisco, and we got along famously. In fact, we're going to bid to fly together next month. We had a great time in Okinawa having steam baths and massages, having our hair done, shopping at the PX, having dinner at the officers' club, etc. etc.

Flying the Pacific is such a nice change from flying to Europe. The weather is lovely everywhere we go, the service on the airplane is really simple, all one class of service, no drinks, just dinner, no choice of entrée, and the troops are really nice, polite passengers—and so easy to please. Going over they're in a fun, adventuresome mood. But, as you might expect, they're pretty quiet on their way home.

Love, Love, Love—
Christine

January 6, 1967

Hi, Mary—

Did I tell you I'm flying military charters to Saigon now? Actually, starting January 2 we're flying into Bien Hoa instead of Saigon. Apparently they moved the reassignment center, or whatever it is. Before our first flight into Bien Hoa the whole crew had a briefing in Okinawa given by a military official, and he told the pilots not to fly over Laos or Cambodia, because they would shoot at us (!). So, when we go there, we fly really high and then take a nose dive into Bien Hoa, let off the troops, board the troops who are going home, and take off straight up (sort of). TWA gives us each an extra whopping $12 hazard pay each time we go in there. Ha.

My last trip the crew was invited to the club at the Marine base, and I met a major who is the quintessential tall, dark and soooo handsome. I'm going to see him again next trip. Can't wait! Romance beckons!

Jason Saga Revisited: Surprise! This morning I got a letter (a first!) from the Beloved One. Be still my heart!!! It was dated 12/23, saying he would like to take me to dinner, but my number is unlisted, so why don't I give him a call, since he can't call me. So, I plan to call him forthwith and posthaste. It's been almost a year!

Love,
Chris

January 30, 1967

Hi, Mums and Daddy –

Did I tell you that the lease is up on Upton Downs, and the landlord is raising the rent? I've been dreading going out into the cold cruel world to apartment hunt, but it turned out to be as easy as walking right next door, which is exactly what I did. My new apartment is pretty much the same as my old one—same rent—and I still have to walk up three flights, BUT it's on the front of the building, so I have a view! Of the street! And, I have some recessed book shelves! (I'm not impervious to these little luxuries, you know.) It's a two-year lease but has a sublet clause after one year. I've dubbed it Upton View, for obvious reasons.

I'm just loving the Pacific flights. Among all the other reasons, one of the best is that we get some nice fat healthy expense checks. The only problem being that when you get back home, your body has been through 12 times zones and back, and it just sleeps for about four days, no matter how much you prod it and poke it and feed it health food and try to shame it into getting out of bed. I truly believe the earth could quake, the government could collapse, and disease could decimate the populace, but the body could still not be roused.

Love, Love, Love—
Christine

January 30, 1967

Hi, Mary—

Just got back from another Viet Nam trip—spent all three evenings of our layover in Okinawa with my darkly handsome Marine. I got to wear a zingy new dress that I bought in Honolulu, so it was doubly fun. It's really a great trip except the part when we fly in and out of Bien Hoa—the hellhole that we have come to know and love.

My supervisor called me before my last trip to inform me that my lost suitcase had finally turned up and that they had it in the hostess office. Apparently, I went in one direction, and it went in another—to Rome, as a matter of fact. When I went out to the hangar and picked it up, I took a firm stand, chastising it severely for going off into the world on its own like that and told it that next time it had an urge to go to Rome, that I would take it there myself. I could hardly have been more forthright. I think I sensed a modicum of shame in its demeanor as it accompanied me home.

Ciao—
Chris
P. S. Flew with funny Joan again recently. She says she really likes Pierre Salinger—he's so lifelike.

February 17, 1967

Hi, Folks—

I'm in the middle of making a sort of abortive attempt at baking oatmeal cookies—the first batch came out a rich jet black color and smoked up the whole apartment, and the second batch looks like a bunch of miniature pancakes. The third batch is in the oven, and I'm looking forward to increasingly better results. (Ralph used to tell me that when I'm in the kitchen, I adopt the scorched earth policy.)

This year my birthday fell in the middle of a Bien Hoa trip, and it started out to be great fun. We deadheaded to SFO on a regularly scheduled flight, and it turns out that the service on coast-to-coast flights is now almost as elaborate as on the international flights to Europe. So, I sat in First Class, feasting on champagne and Chateaubriand and watching the movie—happily playing the role of a First Class passenger to the hilt, gorging and swilling with the best of them. I love my job.

I moved into Upton View on the 3rd. They painted on the 1st and varnished the floor on the 2nd, which I'm told sends the cockroaches scurrying off to the neighboring apartments for a while. Sorry, neighbors.

Love, Love, Love—
Christine

February 17, 1967

Aloha, Mary—

Thanx for the funny birthday card. I had to work really hard on my actual birthday. I was on a Viet Nam trip, and that day we went from Okinawa to Bien Hoa and back, and when it was over, I just wanted to collapse in my hotel room. But, the purser insisted on buying me a birthday drink in the hotel bar, which turned out to be a stellar idea—I ended up having six.

That was the same trip I broke it off with my darkly handsome Marine. What could have been a perfectly lovely relationship was spoiled by the disquieting news that he is dating a school teacher there—and has a wife and three kids in California! A most objectionable man.

On the way home we had three days in Honolulu, and it rained all three. *Quel domage.*

The Jason Saga continues: After about a year, I was reunited with The Beloved One last Friday night. One year has done nothing to alter my view - the attraction (on my part) is stronger than ever. He said some very encouraging words—for straight-laced Jason, that is. Happiness reigns!

Love,
Chris
P.S. On that date I tried wearing false eyelashes for the first time. The next day I found one attached to my shoe, and I never did find the other one.

March 7, 1967

Hi, Mums and Daddy—

No time to write much—I'm leaving for Honolulu in a few minutes. We had two days here in SFO this time, so last night Susanne, Judy and I had dinner and saw the movie, **Georgy Girl**, and then I stayed the night with Susanne so that we could have our compulsory all-night blab-fest. Today was a gorgeous day—sunny and warm—so we went to the park and swang (swung? swinged?) on the swings.

It was nothing to write home about, and yet, here I am writing home about it.

Be sure to read the very interesting article in the Match 31 issue of *Time* magazine. It mentions that they are working on a "beep beep" type of radar for airplanes—like they have in submarines.

Time to saddle up and hit the trail.

Love, Love, Love—
Christine
P.S. I flew with funny Joan again recently. She was trying to tell a passenger who was in conversation with his seat mate, to fasten his seat belt, when he said, "Don't interrupt me when I'm talking!" She answered, "But that's the best time."

March 29, 1967

Dear Mary—

Thank goodness my friend Joan (of "busting out all over fame") is flying the Viet Nam trips, too. She never disappoints. Here are some of her gems:

When I told her I broke up with my Marine, she said, "Don't worry—you can find another man—almost anywhere men are found." She advised me to "be kind to animals and little children—or those who act like them." And, on one flight when I noticed her sitting down, I asked her if she was tired, and she replied, "No—just relaxing between rounds." Then she told me to, "Drink lots of liquids—it's so hard to drink anything else."

And once, when our flight was delayed, she told a passenger that the pilot had misplaced the keys to the airplane. And that before we leave he has to go down and make sure all the tires are pointed in the same direction. (She refers to the pilot as "Beer Breath.")

At one point I overheard a passenger asking her what she called herself—she said "I never have to—I'm always here."

She's an original.

Love,
Chris

May 10, 1967

Hi, Parents—

Here's the lowdown on company passes. I know I've already told you about it on the phone, but now you'll have it on paper for future reference when you travel.

Passes, which are space available, are good from October 15—May 15. Half fares (you pay half of the highest coach fare) are positive space and can be used any time of the year. Quarter fares (you pay 25% of the fare) are positive space eastbound August 1—April 15 and westbound October 15—July 31, or space available eastbound April 16—July 31, and westbound August 1—October 14. There. Crystalline clear, huh?

No, Mom, I've heard nothing from or about Ralph. I'm happy with the way things turned out—no hard feelings. I think of him occasionally, but they're not often charitable thoughts.

More excitement! Last month I was on a layover in Athens, when from my hotel room I thought I heard the sound of airplanes flying close. I was right. When I looked out the window, I saw some small jets (fighter planes?) flying really low, buzzing the street in front of the hotel. Just then the phone rang, and it was the front desk. They were calling all the guests telling us not to leave our rooms until further notice. That "further notice" lasted that day and the next, so as a result we got home a day late. Apparently, there was a coup that day by the military against the current regime. I'm not sure of the outcome.

Love, Love, Love—
Christine

May 10, 1967

Hi, Mary—

Jason Saga Continued: The Beloved Object of my Desire is back in my life! Here's how: I was commiserating with Katy the other night, and she suggested I send him a cute contemporary "I miss you" card, and then I remembered that his birthday was last month, so I sent him a funny belated birthday card. So, glory be (!), last night he called and asked me out for a few beers. (As I was agreeing to the date in modulated tones, inside my head I was screaming YES YES YES!) We had a splendid time—actually necked a bit—and we have a date for the night after I get back from my next trip. My euphoria has persisted all day today.

Had an impromptu house guest the other night. I didn't want to murder him (non-combatant that I am), but there didn't seem to be any other way. I don't think murder is considered a sin if the murderee is a possibly man-eating cockroach, do you?

Ciao—
Chris
P.S. We had a lady on flight from Trinidad the other day. Joan said to her, "Oh, I've been to Trinidad. I threw up in Trinidad. But then, I've thrown up all over the world."

June 21, 1967

Dear Parents—

Last week I had a 4-day layover in Frankfurt, so one of the days I flew over to Berlin to do some sightseeing. I took a tour of West Berlin in the A.M. and one of East Berlin via Checkpoint Charlie in the afternoon. I didn't find East Berlin nearly as dismal as we are led to believe. The people looked quite well dressed, and they have some lovely new shops and hotels. Of course, I realize that you can't tell what their lives are like just by driving by in a bus. East Berlin seems to have been left with the majority of the buildings that weren't bombed during the war, so I found that there was a lot more to see there than in West Berlin.

On the morning tour I sat next to a black U.S. serviceman who was in uniform, and he was quite fun to talk to. He said the Germans were so unused to seeing black people, that when he went to the zoo, he thought the people gawked at him as much as they did the animals.

Love, Love, Love—
Christine
P.S. Oh Woe! We're losing our Pacific charter flights—I'm devastated!

June 21, 1967

Hi, Mary—

My sister Ann's second son Kevin, who is 7 now, just sent me a thank-you note for a birthday present I sent him. He ended the note by saying that, "Second grade is going very well." Isn't that a scream?

Susanne is transferring to JFK in September! Oh joy! Ecstatic as I am about it, that will leave no one in the SFO faction to visit. Apparently, Dyan has moved back to England, and Judy, who is too tall to be a hostess, and who got too tired of hearing about our travels, has joined the State Department and is now based in Munich. (When she told me, my first question was, "When can I visit?") She has a very responsible, but difficult, job—every day she interviews people to decide who gets a visa to visit the U.S., but she has to do it all in German. But then apparently, she has a cute, tall, blond German boyfriend's shoulder to cry on.

Jason Saga continues: I've been out with The Beloved One three times since my last letter. And, quite a bit of kissage occurred!! Seems my romance is rebudding. However, his brother is being ordained as a priest this week, so he told me, in a proper tone of reverential anticipation, that he would be busy for a week with all the relatives from out of town.

Love,
Chris
P.S. We're losing our Pacific flights—much lamenting!

July 22, 1967

Aloha, Mums and Daddy—

Oh woe! My heart is well and truly broken. Our base has lost our beloved Pacific trips! The Company, in all its blithering idiocy, is opening up an International base in SFO to fly the military charters, rather than deadheading us to the coast to cover those flights to Bien Hoa. For about a minute and a half I considered transferring to the new base, but it would really be bad timing. Susanne, who has become my best friend, is transferring to New York International in September, and that means we could bid to fly together to Europe, which would be the (next) best of all possible worlds. Also, rumor has it that the company might be opening up an International base in LAX to fly commercial flights to Hong Kong and Bangkok. Permission to fly that route is up before the CAB now, and if it goes through, I will be the first in line, begging on my knees to transfer there and fly those flights. And I hope Suz will be the second.

My last Bien Hoa flight was at the end of June, so to celebrate our last night on the Pacific run, the whole crew went out together in Honolulu and commiserated by having a delectable prime rib dinner. It was a delightful evening, but sad, overall. Mired in self-pity and Mai Tais, we all agreed that we deplore this wretched turn of events and will desperately miss our layovers in SFO, HNL and Okinawa. Our affair with the Pacific has gone cold.

Love, Love, Love—
Christine

July 22, 1967

Aloha, Mary—

My heart has been utterly broken, and not by any male. We at JFK International have lost our Pacific military charters to a new base opening up in SFO. Devastating news, don't you agree? Of course, I could always transfer there, but the dating scene is 1,000% better in New York.

One of my last trips on the Pacific I had the best layover I've ever had since I started flying. And believe it or not, it was in Okinawa. One of the hostesses on our crew was dating a Marine there, so she fixed the rest of us up with Marines, and the whole group went swimming, water skiing, drinking, dining and dancing every night. My date was a fighter pilot, whose words left no loophole for misunderstanding—he had a wife and 6 kids at home. Too bad—he was gorgeous and lots of fun. I really liked everyone in the group and had the best time ever. I figured out that on that 10-day trip I lost the equivalent of 5 nights' sleep, the result of which was a bad cold that I'm just getting over.

Jason Saga: Went out with Himself on Tuesday night. He told me I looked very pretty, which is unusual for him - compliments don't exactly spring lightly from his lips. Also, at one point he actually referred to me as his girlfriend! Nevertheless, I guess I've given up on the idea of trying to snag him—it's just too discouraging. I suspect he'll still be calling me for dinner once a week—with the perfunctory kiss goodnight—when we're 95 years old.

Love,
Chris

August 14, 1967

Dear Parents—

No, Mom, we can't just take our vacations whenever we want to. Toward the end of each year we bid for them for the following year. Most of the vacations are awarded during the times of the year when the loads are lightest—mine is in November again this year, and I'm probably going to East Africa on a photographic safari with the English girl that I went to South America with.

I'm flying to Frankfurt this month, and my last trip had a two-day layover, so a few of us took a boat trip down the Rhine and saw lots of castles on hills. It always amazes me when other tourists are so busy looking through their viewfinders and clicking away, that they're not really drinking in the scenery. I guess they drink it in when they get home and have their pictures developed.

August 28, 1967

Hello again—

Just came across this letter, which I thought I mailed two weeks ago. In the meantime I've met a new guy—his name is Peter, and he's a detective for the NYPD. He is extremely good looking, in a dark, Italian sort of way, and is great fun on top of it. We went out twice last week, and he says that he loves the theater, so I'm looking forward to seeing lots of plays with him.I suspect you'll probably be hearing more about him—we really clicked. The game is afoot!

Love, Love, Love—
Christine

August 28, 1967

Dear Mary—

"I was strolling in the park one day..." tra la la—Central Park Zoo, that is, when I happened to strike up a conversation with a handsome stranger. He asked me how I was, I told him how I was, and we went from there. His name, I subsequently found out is Peter, and he is a detective for the NYPD. Well, he is no longer a stranger. We went out twice last week and had great fun, and next week we're going bicycling in Central Park. Actually, he's a little too good looking for my taste—also not overly educated, and not what you might call a deep thinker, but he has lots of street smarts. He's perfect for those dry periods when Jason doesn't call. I can't see this romance lasting all that long, but it seems like a "wonderful fling to be flung."

Jason Saga: Went out with The Beloved One once this week, and at one point he told me that I'm "hard to get." (ME? Is he KIDDING?) I guess he means that he calls a lot when I'm out on flight. Serves him right for calling on the spur of the moment. On my part, I've cultivated the habit of patient expectancy.

Love,
Chris

September 27, 1967

Dear Folks—

No, I haven't read *The Arrangement*, Mom, but I will add that to my endless list. At the moment I'm rereading *Dr. Zhivago*, after seeing the movie with Peter, who (whom?) has quickly become a constant in my life. We just can't seem to see enough of each other. He even runs over to see me for 15 minutes after work and before his classes. (He's taking courses in Speech, Drama, and Police Science.) We celebrated his birthday last week by going to see *Black Comedy* on Broadway. Then Saturday we saw *The Apple Tree*, and that night I made his favorite food—steaks and French fries—and baked a chocolate birthday cake. And, Voila! I broke a lifelong habit by making everything (while not by any means *haute cuisine*) totally edible! Will miracles never cease?

Sunday we took a walk in Central park—he always carries a gun, so I feel very safe wherever we go. Then we spent the afternoon at the Metropolitan Museum and then saw two horror movies and had hamburgers and drank beer. We have so much fun doing nothing together. It's glorious to be in love again! Sort of. (Sort of in love, not sort of glorious).

Love, Love, Love—
Christine

September 27, 1967

Hi, Mary—

Jason Saga—The Conclusion: Wherein He Leaves Center Stage:

Himself called me to go out three times last week, and—get ready for this—I actually turned him down three times. Only a short month ago I was a slavering Jason worshiper, and now he seems to be receding into my dim, blurry past. (Sounds like bad novel talk, huh?) Goodbye, Mystery Man! Are you married? Are you gay? I'll never know.

I am really wild about my handsome detective! Last week we went to the wedding of a friend of his, and at the reception he proposed to me. I told him to sober up. During the reception, which was held in the bride's apartment, one of the male guests, who had had an unspecified number of glasses of champagne, disappeared into the bedroom for quite some time and then emerged dressed in the bride's negligee. The bride was not amused.

Here's an interesting observation Peter made in a more somber moment the other day, which may explain our different outlooks. He says that in my job I see people at their best—they're going on vacation, so they're happy and eager for new adventures, whereas, in his job he sees people at their worst, after they've been raped, robbed or beaten up or whatever. Are we drawn to our jobs because of that? Or, do our jobs make us what we are? Or, is this more bad-novel talk?

Love,
Chris

October 23, 1967

Hi, Folks -

I'm flying a great rotation this month—2 trips to Madrid, and 2 trips in which we work to Athens, lay over a day there, deadhead to Paris, have a day there, and work home. I'm flying with the two girls I went to South America with last year, one of which I'm going on vacation to Africa with after this trip. I'm in Athens now. We get back to New York at 1:00 P.M. on Thursday, so if I can make it to the Annual Emergency Training at the hangar by 1:30, then we may be able to leave for Africa on Friday, and if not, then we will leave on Sunday. All this excessive detail is to let you know when to start worrying, Mom. This year you have a whole new set of worries—about my perhaps being gored by a rhino, crushed by an anaconda, or even torn apart by a rogue lion. Or, possibly being brought low by a bout of Dengue fever. Or, more likely, trampled by gangs of tourists, wild-eyed with picture-snapping panic.

I bought scads of film for the photo safari. A girl I'm flying with went there last year, and she took 400 pictures!

Did I tell you that we recently got a new contract, and I got a $35 a month raise? And, we'll get another raise next year. Peter has forced me to explore the too-often ignored subject of $, or more accurately, the lack thereof. He has figured out a budget for me, so that perhaps I may be operating in the black at some point within this epoch.

Love, Love, Love—
Christine

October 23, 1967

Mary, M'dear—

Bulletin from the front! Unless I have a compelling reason not to, I can now keep flying until I'm 60 years old! With our new contract the company rescinded the age 35 mandatory retirement rule, so though I never intended to make flying my life's work, fate may decree otherwise. While it's not a career, it certainly is a lifestyle that I would be hard put to give up.

We still have the no-longer-than-chin-length hair rule, but Suz tells me that lots of girls on Domestic wear wigs on flight and have long hair of their own underneath. So, I bought a blond wig in Madrid, and I'm letting my own locks grow freely. I find, though, that while wigs are nice and warm in cold weather, I have limited endurance for the pressure they put on the noggin. Ow!

Peter and I are still going strong. Last week we went to a Broadway play called **The Homecoming** and also to the Moscow Circus at Madison Square Garden. I've noticed that he seems to like it when I'm quiet—he thinks I'm listening.

Well, it's 6:00 A.M., and I have to get up at 8:00 A.M. to deadhead to Paris, so I guess I'll rack up some zees. *Viva la France!*

Adieu—
Chris

November 18, 1967

Hi, Parents—

Did you get all my postcards from Africa? What a fantastic experience it was! Here's a rundown: We started out in Nairobi and from there took a photo safari to a nearby game park and saw more different animals there in the wild than anywhere else on our trip—so many that I can't even begin to name them all. Well, okay – I'll give it a whirl: elephants, lions, lots of zebras, giraffes, one cheetah, a hippo, some rhinos, eland, ostrich, and roughly 1,000,000 Thompson gazelles. I think most of my pictures, though, are of animals' rear ends because they tend to run away when you come near them. (I found the striped zebra behinds to be the most picturesque.)

We spent a night at Treetops, which is a lodge built about 40 feet up in a tree and sits next to a watering hole/ salt lick. which is lit up at night, when all sorts of animals come to be ogled and snapped by tourists who are on the roof porch of the lodge, whispering and going stocking footed, so as not to scare them away. (After several gin and tonics, it becomes increasingly difficult to stay quiet.) We could see the remains of the original Treetops across the way, where Princess Elizabeth was staying with Prince Philip in 1952 when she found out her father had died and that she was now the queen.

Then we spent a couple of nights at a lodge on the rim of Ngorongoro Crater, which we were told is the largest (100 square miles) inactive, unfilled volcanic crater in the world. Riding down the 2,000 feet to the crater floor takes forever, but the view itself is unforgettable—well worth the bumpy jeep ride. When we finally got down to the bottom, we saw some lions eating a freshly caught animal of some sort, and we were told that, although the females make the kill, the male eats first, and the females and cubs get the leftovers. The animals share the crater with the very picturesque Masai tribesmen who walk around, each armed with a long, heavy spear, taller than they are.

Dar Es Salaam, in Tanzania, is a whole different world—has more of an Arabian feel than Kenya. The shopping there is extensive, except that everything is made out of dead animals. We flew over to Zanzibar for one day—it's an all-Muslim island—seemed very exotic to us. The whole island smells of spices—the nostrils' delight!

On our way home we stopped in Ethiopia (Addis Ababa) for a couple of days. We walked by the palace where Haile Sellassie lives, then walked through a very primitive village and really got stared (and glared) at. They obviously don't get many Western tourists there. And, we got the feeling that it was fine with them.

My esteemed colleague, Helen, was a delightful travel partner and is a lovely and fun person. And she never complained. She left that part up to me. I can do that. It is well within my scope.

Love, Love, Love—
Christine
P. S. Did you know that a group of hippopotamuses is called a "bloat?" Me, neither. And, rhinoceroses are a "crash." And, giraffes are a "tower." That one fits.

November 19, 1967

Hi, Mary—

Just got back from Africa—racked up quite a few memorable moments to add to my ever-increasing collection. The first one happened on the second leg of the trip, when I woke up on the airplane and looked out the window at what turned out to be the Great Rift. Nobody announced what we were flying over, so I felt lucky to have awakened just then.

Another one happened while we were waylaid at a small village in Kenya for a few hours, due to a flat tire on our jeep. We were trying to make conversation with the local Masai people by using some words and phrases out of our Berlitz Swahili phrasebook, when it turned out, to our delight, they spoke English quite well—and with an English accent, which is always a surprise to hear coming from natives—who are not natives of England, that is. Anyhow, I remember talking with one very dignified fellow who appeared to be without a nervous system, as there were flies crawling all over him—even in his eyes and mouth—yet he didn't seem to care—or even notice. Not exactly a magical moment, but memorable, nonetheless.

Another moment was at sunset when we were driving out of Ngorongoro Crater, which takes an eon (its 2,000 feet to the bottom) of zigzagging back and forth with ever-widening views of the crater. There were two Masai tribesmen walking on the floor of the crater, but even when they got to be tiny pinpoints in the distance, we could still see the reflection of the setting sun on the long, shiny spears they carried.

Another of the moments was when we were on our photo safari, and we apparently drove too close to a newly laid ostrich egg, so the male ostrich came running at us and slammed his body against the side of our van with an enormous crash. Wasn't that brave of him?

Another one was when we went to Lake Manyara, ostensibly to see lions who hang out in the trees. We saw lots of trees—sans lions. Not one lion. But, we did see hundreds of pink flamingos wading in the lake, and when they all took off in flight at once, it was spectacular.

Not all the memorable moments were positive, though. We were at a shop in Dar Es Salaam where we saw an end table for sale that was made out of the bottom part of an actual elephant's leg. Isn't that appalling?

We spent one night at Treetops, which you've no doubt heard of. Across the salt lick we could see the remains of the original Treetops, where Princess Elizabeth was when she found out that her father had died and she had become queen. Apparently it was burned down during the Mau Mau uprisings in the 1950s.

We had one day in exotic Zanzibar, where we just rode around and saw lots of ornately carved houses on stilts, but I'll never forget the smell that permeates the whole island—it was of cinnamon, cloves and nutmeg all together. Yum!

Oh, I almost forgot—we saw lions doing the deed. It put us all in a giggly mood.

Love,
Chris

December 29, 1967

Hi, folks—

Yes, Mom, I did have to fly on Christmas afternoon, but it was the only rotation I could hold that Peter and I could be together on Christmas Eve and New Year's Eve both. My Christmas trip was to Geneva—my first time there, but it was so miserably cold and dismal that we—the whole crew—just stayed in the hotel and hibernated.

Thanks, again, for the coat and dress you gave me for Christmas. You can be sure I will wear the coat ALL the time. I wore the dress out to dinner at Dawson's Pub with Peter a couple of weeks ago, and he said that I got lots of stares. He is used to getting ogled because of his good looks, so he was jealous, because apparently I got more ogles than he did.

Had an epiphany recently. P loaned me his thermal underwear to wear under my wool pants suit—it was all of 27 degrees out—and for the first time in my life I could actually enjoy walking about in the freezing weather because I wasn't cold! I could just relax and stroll around like everybody else, without suffering infinite torture!

How I miss those Pacific flights with layovers in the warm, Hawaiian sunshine!

Love, Love, Love—
Chris

December 29, 1967

Hey, Mary—

Hope you are having a splendid holiday. Today I'm in Rome. TWA recently bought Hilton International, so we stay at the Cavalieri Hilton now, which is a lovely hotel, but pretty far from downtown. Besides that, it's cold and damp out, and I really don't like the crew much, so I've just been lolling about in my room, even though I really enjoy interacting with Italians—they are such warm, jolly people. This morning at breakfast the waiter told me that they were serving "fresh smashed orange juice." Isn't that a kick?

No, dearie, I won't be getting serious about Peter. He's actually a wonderful boyfriend except for three major flaws: he has a beastly temper, and he's intensely jealous, which together are a dangerous combination, especially in one who goes around with a gun in his belt at all times. Also, no matter how much I poke and prod him to find a soft spot, I think he is almost totally devoid of tenderheartedness. I've decided that beneath this hostile detective's exterior lies a hostile detective's interior.

Common sense dictates that I should RUN. But, I'm going to take my time about it.

Happy New Year—
Chris

January 24, 1968

Greetings, Esteemed Parents—

Just reread the last letter you wrote, Mom, after you got home from visiting Ann. You mentioned how tired you were, and I think I believe you—you spelled Kenny with three Ns. Ha!

It is miserably cold here in New York now—0 degrees last night. Apropos of the weather, we ventured out to see the Ice Follies at Madison Square Garden and also the movie *In Cold Blood*. Tomorrow night we're going to poke our noses out of our burrows long enough see the play *Mame*, which has nothing to do with cold, but maybe we'll be so engrossed in the play that we will forget about the weather for a split second. The only thing getting me through this horribly cold, miserable month is contemplating our upcoming vacation. Did I tell you that P and I are going to Trinidad and Tobago for a few days for my birthday? I ache for that sunshine!

Well, after a few successes, I seem to have fallen back into my failure-in-the-kitchen mode. Recently I took a stab at fudge making—Peter said they tasted like chocolate-covered sawdust. Then I tried making some ice box cookies, but when I went to slice the dough, it fell apart. Do you suppose it could be because I had the dough in the freezer for three weeks? I bow to your superior knowledge in these matters.

Love, Love, Love—
Christine

January 24, 1968

Hey, Mary, M'dear—

Did you have a fun New Year's Eve? Peter and I had a quiet one—stayed home in Upton View and watched the new TV that P bought me for Christmas and shared a bottle of champagne, which we weren't even in the mood for. Actually, we were recovering from the night before, when we went to Chateau Madrid, which is a fancy Spanish restaurant with a Flamenco dancing show.

For my birthday this year P and I are going to Trinidad and Tobago—Trinidad for shopping and sightseeing, and Tobago for lolling on the beach. The latter is rumored to be the most like the South Seas of any island in the Caribbean. Too, too romantic, huh?

I've saved the most exciting news for last. We're getting new uniforms! And, apparently they are going to be very fashion forward (not quite haute couture, but as close to it as we'll ever get). It consists of a dress and jacket combo, A-line, double knit, in a choice of orange, yellow or green, white patent leather boots, skirts 3 inches above the knee, and best of all—NO hats!!

Happiness reigns!

Love,
Chris

February 22, 1968

Hi, Mums and Daddy—

Thanks 1,000,000 for the birthday check. I intended to spend it in Trinidad, but the shopping there was woefully disappointing. Actually, the whole vacation was a colossal disappointment. We both had the flu (or, more likely, food poisoning), and it rained incessantly in both Trinidad and Tobago, so we took evasive action and spent the last week in Barbados. But, at least we were able to avoid the zero cold weather and garbage strike in New York City, so it wasn't a total waste.

Yes, Mom that was my yearly vacation. I get 15 days, but by bidding adeptly, I managed to get 25 days. We were on a 17-day excursion fare, so that was as long as we could stay; however, that was more than sufficient, as it turned out.

In answer to my plea, Ann sent me her "never fail" fudge recipe. In it, the directions say, "boil until soft ball stage." What the heck is a "soft ball stage???"

Love, Love, Love—
Christine

February 22, 1968

Hi, Mary—

An apt description of our vacation to Trinidad and Tobago would be that, "a good time was NOT had by all." To say that we argued unceasingly would not be an exaggeration. Apparently, it was my fault that the shopping was uninspiring, that it rained incessantly and that we both got the flu (or maybe it was food poisoning—either way, it was my fault). Trinidad and Tobago are touted as a "sunlover's heaven." There was nothing missing there except the sun—and maybe heaven. Of course, Peter's passion for complaining never waned.

At some point we managed to agree on one thing long enough to invest in adjoining property lots in the Bahamas, which seemed like a good idea at the time. The payments are only $15 a month (I assume that will be for the rest of my natural life). Good move or bad? Whatcha think?

On a lighter note—on my last flight before vacation we had the Director of Dining Services on board. I'm not sure where he's from, but he has an unusual accent—he suggested that I take the "asparagoose" out of the "orphan" (oven) a little sooner. When we served Prosciutto and Melon as the first course in First Class, he told me to make a note on the flight report that the prosciutto was limp. Later on, when I was in the cockpit, the captain asked me how the DDS was doing, so I told him that he had complained that the prosciutto was limp, and the captain said, "What's he doing with his prosciutto out in flight, anyway?"

Ta Ta—
Chris

216

March 26, 1968

Dear Parents—

I'm sorry to hear you had to pay 4 cents postage due on my last letter. Hope you thought it was worth it.

I cajoled Peter into going with me to the Flower Show at the Coliseum recently. He hates flowers. (Does anybody else in the wide world hate flowers?) I thought it would be like a breath of spring—to temporarily, at least, deliver us from the cold, filthy, dismal atmosphere of New York City. But it failed to do the trick. Then we went to see *The Graduate*, which is the best movie I've seen in months, and which took us out of our depressing surroundings for a couple of hours.

Yes, Mom, I would love to go to Rome with you in the fall. Wanna include Madrid? Or Athens? Or Cairo? October sounds just dandy. The small fry are back in school, crowds have dwindled, weather still nice. A stellar idea.

The Sunday before last we ventured out and walked up to Fifth Avenue to watch the St. Patrick's Day Parade. P enjoyed it only because he got to boo Bobby Kennedy, who was marching in the parade, so that made him happy (P, not Bobby Kennedy).

Love, Love, Love—
Christine

March 26, 1968

Hi, Mary—

I'm in Milan this week—traded into it, and last week I traded into a Frankfurt trip. It was a pleasure to go someplace different after three months of flying to Rome. The company, in all its (non)wisdom had seen fit to inflict on us a 3-month bid period on a trial basis, which pleased nobody and aggravated everybody. I didn't think I would mind it, but I found that, not only is it fiendishly complicated to bid for three months at a time, but it does get tiresome flying the same flight and working with the same crew for three months straight. Fortunately, the union was able to negotiate one-month bid periods for us from now on.

No, Mom, I haven't read *The Graduate* yet, but it is on my ever-lengthening list. Lately I've been reading the short stories of Hemingway and O. Henry. Short stories seem to work well for the shorter attention span needed while on the road.

We saw two movies last week—one good and one not good. I won't tell you about the not-so-good one, lest you be biased beforehand. The good one (actually REALLY good) was, *The Good, The Bad and The Ugly.* I predict you'll just love it. I did.

I've written a poem to express my present mood. It goes: Bring spring!

Love, Chris

April 17, 1968

Hi, Mums and Daddy—

What luck! This month I was able to hold a bid that has always gone very senior before. It goes to Paris, with a short layover there—only long enough to get a good night's sleep. We fly two days and then have four off for the whole month, and it has 10 hours of overtime. Love my job!

Peter and I have done a couple of interesting things lately—went to the North American Karate Championship Match at the new Madison Square Garden, which I found mildly entertaining. But, then we went to the races! I'd never been to a horse race before, so I studied in depth the sheets they give you with all the horse info and the odds and what not. The first horse I picked was named "Ragamuffin" and had 20-1 odds, which I figured would win me pots of money. When the gun went off, he shot out ahead of the other horses and stayed in the lead for the whole first half of the race. I was SO excited! I had no trouble identifying him at the end of the race—he was the one that came in trailing after all the others—dead last - as a result of which I lost $2.

I've decided the whole racing industry is fraught with peril—just going out of its way to confuse the innocent bystander.

Love, Love, Love—
Christine
P.S. Spring is finally here—when a young girl's fancy lightly turns to thoughts of new clothes.

April 17, 1968

Dear Mary—

Wasn't it just horrible about Martin Luther King? Ever since he was shot, we see policemen on every corner of the city— in bunches—with crash helmets on. Apparently, the police are working 12-hour days and 6 days a week, because they are expecting riots. But, so far all's quiet on the Eastern front.

Now, dearie, I have a big not-to-be-divulged secret for your ears only. P and I decided last night to get married as soon as he has saved $5,000. He seems to think he needs that much for a ring and for the Honeymoon to Surpass all Honeymoons. So, if we don't break up before then (which is always a distinct possibility) it will probably happen in the summer.

Flew with my busty blond friend Joan again. She describes her latest boyfriend as "simple, yet satisfying." And, she described one of our passengers as "the human equivalent of a storm cloud." He had said to her, "I don't complain." And then he proceeded to do so. He kept inflicting on her his momentously important opinions, so she finally excused herself from him by saying she had to go into the cockpit and wake up the crew. (She addresses the captain as "your pilotness," or the more informal, "milord.")

Love,
Chris

May 23, 1968

Hi, You Two—

Have you ever traveled without a suitcase? What a wonderfully free feeling! Susanne and I flew to San Francisco recently for a day of shopping—out in the morning—back that night. We didn't buy much, but we had a blissful day of uninterrupted conversing. We'll be working trips together before long—Suz has her transfer in for New York International, so then we will be able to bid to fly together.

Peter has been relentlessly clever in coming up with ideas about things for us to do. (Once his brain gets cranked up, there's no stopping it.) Last week we went to a great Czechoslovakian restaurant and then saw the play *The Odd Couple* at Radio City—sooooo funny! The next day we went to the Aquarium at Coney Island and watched them feed the killer whale. This week we saw the movie *2001* and the play *How Now Dow Jones* and went to the circus in the new Madison Square Garden. That was the first American circus I had ever seen, and it was quite the extravaganza.

I'm on a layover in Frankfurt now, and I hear the birdies beginning to chirp, so I guess I'd better nod off for a few hours before crew call.

Love, Love, Love—
Christine

May 23, 1968

Mary, Dear –

Read this attentively:

You absolutely must run out this minute and pick up a copy of **Let's Eat Right to Keep Fit** by Adele Davis. I'm not at all sure how I happened onto it, but it's fascinating, life-changing, can't-put-down reading. It's all about how different vitamins and minerals work in the bod, info with which heretofore I had not the remotest acquaintance. Which is a pretentious way of saying that I've been living on "junk food," a term apparently coined by Adele Davis' cook.

So, as a result, Peter and I are on a pretty intense health kick. P bought me a blender to make us health drinks with Tiger's Milk, yeast, etc. Last week I made some wheat germ muffins that we both gagged on, and this week I made a loaf of whole wheat bread that P said looked like an elephant turd.

Love,
Chris
P. S. Today is Buddha's birthday—just thought you ought to know.

June 20, 1968

Hi, Parents—

Good news! Susanne's transfer did in fact come through in time for us to bid together for this month. It's called "buddy bidding," and we were able to hold the same rotation.

A most fortuitous thing happened to us on our trip to Athens a couple of weeks ago. Early one evening we were walking down from the Acropolis, and we passed by an old Roman outdoor amphitheater, which is still in use—it's called the Theater of Herod Atticus. We noticed that some people were walking down into it and sitting there as though there was going to be a performance, so we sat ourselves down to see what was happening. Turns out the performance was something I'll never ever forget. It was actually Pablo Casals in person conducting at a performance of an oratorio that he wrote called El Pesebre (The Peace). It was a warm evening, and while we sat there the sun went down, and it was SO beautiful—just magical.

You know, things like this often happen when Suz and I get together. There seems to be some kind of good-luck energy working for the two of us that's always a surprise. We've often commented on the fact that when we're together parking places magically appear, great things to do pop up out of nowhere, flights we wouldn't have made are delayed—stuff like that. So, it's a very special kind of friendship.

Love, Love, Love—
Christine

June 20, 1968

Oh, Mary, I just finished your book, and it was absolutely brilliant!!! I loved the snappy, can't-fall-asleep language. I'm buying copies for all my family and friends. I'm so proud of you! And proud to be your friend! Does this mean you're smarter than I am? I hate that.

Peter was very favorably impressed, too, and he has never been one to pay felonious compliments. Have you started writing another one yet?

Peter and I came perilously close to breaking up this week. We had a trial separation after one of his famous fits of anger. It lasted one day (the separation—not the fit of anger—the fit of anger went on for about a week).

I had thought it wouldn't be too difficult to break up with him, but I couldn't eat or sleep that day, so I guess I'm hooked! All is well now, and he's talking about getting married before January, so we can take a vacation to Florida and the Bahamas to see the lots we're buying. It may just happen that way—I wouldn't rule it out altogether. On the other hand...

Love,
Chris

July 22, 1968

Hi, Parents—

Did I tell you that Susanne and I are flying together again this month? A very interesting thing happened to us on a layover in Rome while we were sitting, in the late afternoon, at a table around the pool of the Cavalieri Hilton. We were in the midst of having cocktails and engrossed in our never-ending blabfest, when an Arab man walked over to us and asked us to leave the pool area because it was being closed so that King Saud could have a swim. So, before we could gather up our things, out sauntered King S. surrounded by his entourage, and not 20 feet from us he promptly dropped his white robe and lowered himself into the pool and splashed around for a while and then left us - to milk whatever we could from the moment.

I think I can say without fear of contradiction that I'll probably never again have the dubious pleasure of being quite that close to a king in his swimming trunks. And, I must say that he looked quite fit for a man in his late 60s.

Love, Love, Love—
Christine

July 22, 1968

Dear Mary—

Flew with my dumb-like-a-fox friend Joan again recently. More gems: She told me that after boarding she had gone down the checklist and that there was indeed the obligatory crying baby on board. And, she said of one of the more odious passengers that she recognized she was in the presence of immeasurable stupidity, because he was operating "without benefit of brain." Her barbs do not exclude crew members. She said of a fellow hostess, "She hates compliments like boats hate water." Ha! And, she reminded me to genuflect before I go into the cockpit and to be sure to leave the cockpit walking out backwards, bowing my way out.

Peter and I spent last weekend at Seaside Heights in New Jersey. They have a lovely big beach there and a boardwalk with rides like Coney Island has. The weather was hazy, but hot, and we managed to get a little sun on our hitherto lily-white bods. We only fought once or twice, so we had a pretty good time. I spent most of the time, however, fantasizing about hitting him over the head with a surf board.

You can forget anything I ever said about marrying P. Too much dissension. Padded cells were invented for people like him. I've decided to bid longer trips so I'm not with him so much.

Love,
Chris

August 16, 1968

Hi, Folks—

Peter and I have had a good week, the highlight of which was definitely seeing **Romeo and Juliet** in Central Park (along with roughly 9 zillion other people). Yesterday we spent the day on Jones Beach and then saw **South Pacific** at the Jones Beach Theater last night.

Must hasten to tell you how delighted I am that you two are coming to New York City to see me next month! If you can at all help it, try to avoid traveling on passes on a weekend. I'm afraid it's too late to write for tickets to the Johnny Carson Show, but we can go there on the day of the show and stand in line for tickets. Apparently they start taping at 6:00 P.M., and I'm told it shouldn't be a problem getting in.

Looks like Susanne won't be able to do anything with us—she will be "otherwise engaged" while you're here. Her new amour travels on business a lot, and she goes with him whenever she can, so she'll be OOT (out of town) all that week. But P will be ever present. I hope you like him. As I may have pointed out before, reticence is not one of his strong points. I suspect he considers it a day wasted that doesn't contain an argument with somebody or an altercation of some sort or another, so he can rip somebody's head off. Just, of course, kidding.

Love, Love, Love—
Christine

September 3, 1968

Hi, Mary—

News Bulletin: My parents are coming to New York City! Mom has been here before, but this time she has miraculously succeeded in persuading daddy to come along. I suspect that the main—or maybe the only—reason he agreed to come is that he wants to see the Johnny Carson Show live, because they watch it every night at home.

Remember our old friend Judy, who is living in Munich now, working for the Consulate? Well, Friday Susanne and I were on a layover in Frankfurt, so Judy flew over and had dinner with us and spent the night in our hotel. Then, when we left for D.C., she went to Berlin for the weekend. I had almost forgotten how much fun we Three Musketeers used to have when we lived together in SFO.

My schedule for September couldn't be better. I was taken off a trip because I'm high on time for the quarter, so now I get back from a trip on the 15th and don't fly again until the 28th. Now I'll be home for P's birthday – I'm going to take him to see *Man of La Mancha*. We saw *West Side Story* this week. The show was good, but the theater is fantastic—it's in Lincoln Center, which is so beautiful I wanted to squat right down and take up residence there!

Love,
Chris

September 18, 1968

Dear Mums and Daddy—

Susanne and I are having a jolly old time flying together. Earlier this month we had a double crossing—JFK-FRA-DC-FRA-JFK. In D.C. we went to the Smithsonian—spent several hours there and didn't even get through one building. We did manage to see the Hope Diamond, though. Then we went back to the hotel, split a bottle of wine and put the world to rights.

Last month I had a bit of luck—the company gave me a pay assignment for one of my trips, which means that they pay you for the flight but you don't have to go, for one reason or another. I think it must happen once in a millennium. I've been flying 7 1/2 years, and it's a first for me. So, anyhow, I spent three glorious, fun-filled days cleaning out the cupboards and oven of Upton View. So very glamorous, huh?

The weather should be perfect for your visit next week. It has been 80 in the daytime and 60–65 at night, and beautifully sunny. I called Circle Line, and they have boat tours around Manhattan until November 10. Can't wait 'til you get here! As I'm often cautioned—don't fly too close to the sun.

Love, Love, Love—
Christine

September 29, 1968

Hi, Mary—

I'm happy (and relieved) to report that my parents' visit was a rousing success. Peter drove us everywhere in his car, and my dad, who is the quintessential "quiet man" would laugh out loud when P yelled at the other drivers. As I warned them, reticence is not one of P's strengths.

We did in fact get to the Johnny Carson Show. After waiting several years in line, at the very last minute we got seats right down in front. I'm sure that was the highlight of the trip for them.

I'm having a lazy Sunday afternoon in Rome. It's too cool to lie out by the pool, so after demolishing mountains of spaghetti, we all have retired to our respective rooms. I took a nap, and now I'm going to delve into *The Graduate*.

On our flight over yesterday we had two prominent passengers on board in the form of the designers Pucci and Yves St. Laurent. I was working in the back and they, of course, were in First Class, so I didn't get to interact with them. In my section, however, we did have a guy who told me he was on PCP, and as a matter of fact, he did act kind of weird. Sort of gives new meaning to the term "flying high."

Ciao—
Chris

October 28, 1968

Dear Folks—

Not much to report except that Peter and I broke up. I really thought that this time the breakup was for good - and for the best. But, human nature being what it is, we subsequently ceased hostilities and negotiated a peace. I guess we are happier (or probably, less unhappy) together than we are apart.

    Today is the last of 11 days of not working. A week ago Friday I had a wisdom tooth pulled, and as a result I spent a whole week in bed with the pain. I couldn't eat much of anything, so when the pain subsided and it became time to take my trip, I was too weak to function, so I had to go off schedule. I've decided that pain is an unnecessary design flaw. Why not just have a "beep beep" or some such warning to let us know when something is awry?

    I'm flying to Geneva next month so that I can buy P an elegant watch for Christmas. He says he is going to buy me a diamond for Christmas, but he is also going to buy a new car, and he's saving for a honeymoon/vacation, too, so I suspect the more likely scenario would be that the diamond will manifest itself in time for my birthday in February.

Love, Love, Love—
Christine

October 28, 1968

Hi, Mary—

I'm sure you remember "bustin' out all over" Joan, she of the very large forefront. Well, I flew with her again recently, and as you can imagine, my ears were flapping, waiting for one of her priceless *bon mots*. I didn't have to wait long.

We were exchanging boyfriend woes when she said that if her boyfriend got another brain, he'd just have one. Ha! Then she said, "For years I was my own worst critic. Then I met Derek." Later, a passenger gave her his card, on which he was listed as Director of Operations, and she said to him, "Oh, do you work in a hospital then?" At one point she caught someone smoking when the "No Smoking" sign was lit, and she told him that, "There are many reasons for this restriction, but first and foremost among them is the fact that it's forbidden." Then later on in the flight a passenger told her that by soaring to such lofty heights we were defying the Law of Gravity, and she said, "Do you mean that we laugh too much?" The passenger uttered a cordial guffaw and went back to his seat.

I think she's destined to traverse the world delighting everyone.

Love,
Chris

November 3, 1968

Dear Parents—

I'm in Frankfurt now waiting for my crew call, which is ½ hour late already. We were supposed to be home on Friday, but the airplane we were to take home from here didn't get in the night before because of fog, so instead they had us work a flight to Washington D.C. When we got there, they gave us a choice (a first in my experience) of coming home the next morning or working a flight back here to der Fatherland again, and since it meant an extra $160 in overtime, we all chose to work back here.

It was nice to have a day in D.C.—Susanne and I went to the Mint and to the Lincoln Memorial, and when I suggested that we walk to the top of the Washington Monument, to my surprise, she totally agreed with me. So up we trooped—898 steps!

Flying is 1,000,000% more fun when it's done with one's best friend.

Love, Love, Love,
Christine
P.S. Latest joke going around:
Machochist: "Hit me!"
Sadist: "No"

November 6, 1968

Greetings, Mary

This last week has been just frantic—I've been running around like a Keystone Kop in an old-time movie. I had only two days off, in which time I had to do the following: buy material and line a dress I had made, buy a purse and shoes (for P's sister's engagement party on Saturday), have my last fitting and/or pick up a coat I'm having made, buy and send a present to one of Ann's K's, do the laundry, wash my hair, vote, go to the gynecologist and have my cervix cauterized, plus various minor errands which I did this morning—then broke my neck getting to the airport in time for my flight—checked in 2 minutes before the deadline—and the flight CANCELLED!!! And, it was the Geneva flight that I had bid to buy a watch for P for Christmas! Bugger! Bugger! Bugger!

So, they put me on a flight tomorrow night to Rome, and I don't get back until Saturday night. We land at 4:35, and the party is at 7:00—so even if all goes well, I'll be late. On the other hand, if it's a boring party, maybe I'll be glad I'm late.

Love,
Chris

December 27, 1968

My Dear Parents—

Romance and adventure beckon! On January 7 Peter and I will be applying sunscreen to our goosebumps and fleeing the marrow-chilling ice fields of New York, seeking solace on the sunshiny beaches of South Florida. We have 23 glorious days to forget all our cares and woes and concentrate on exchanging our prison pallor for coppery suntans. Oh, joy!

In addition to the mountains of Christmas and vacation-related tasks I have had this month (doing Christmas cards, wrapping and mailing presents, making Christmas cookies, having my picture taken on Santa's lap, etc.), I also had to go apartment hunting. My lease on Upton View is up February 1, and we'll be in Florida in the interim, so I've had to line up something this month.

As Johnny Carson has probably informed you, the weather here has been abominable. P tried to drive me around apartment hunting one day, and when we got out of the car, we walked about a block, and it was so unbelievably cold and windy that we RAN back to the car and scraped the ice off our faces. Besides the intimidating weather, the housing situation looks pretty dismal—seems there is an acute apartment shortage in New York City of late. In order to find one I can afford, I'm going to have to move way uptown to an area called Washington Heights—up by the George Washington Bridge. It's residential, with more trees, less traffic and (almost) no dog poop. I found one that I love (apartment, not dog poop) in a big, modern building with doorman, close access to bus and subway, and a view—sort of.

Love, Love, Love—
Christine

December 27, 1968

Hi, Mary—

I'm in London now on a double crossing—to D.C. tomorrow—then back to FRA—then home again. We left New York last night, and it had snowed all day, so we were delayed 6 hours waiting for the airplane to come in, being de-iced, and waiting our turn to take off—finally got here at 4 A.M—I had been up 28 hours. We were all ready for the infirmary.

Did you have a very merry Christmas? It was too brutally cold and windy in New York to do anything that day, so we just stayed home and made cookies - festooned with candied ginger. Yum! The week before we did venture out to see two Pinter plays—*The Tea Party* and *The Basement*. And on the 23rd we saw *The Nutcracker* ballet at Lincoln Center—sooooo beautiful!

I found a splendid new apartment for when my lease is up in February, but I almost didn't get it. The Superintendent told me I could have it, but when I called back, his wife said they wanted $100 from me or they would give it to someone else. It was not her lucky day. P called her back and informed her that kickbacks are illegal and that if she persisted he would turn her in, so I got the apartment. As you may have guessed, dear reader, P is not just a pretty face.

Love,
Chris

January 30, 1969

Greetings, Esteemed Parents –

I would give our vacation to Miami about a 6 on a 1-10 scale—only because we had a scant five days of sunshine. In spite of the rain, we did go to Monkey Jungle, the Serpentarium, the Seaquarium, the Wax Museum, went on a boat tour of the Everglades, to the dog races and to Jai Alai, went deep sea fishing (I caught a barracuda) and saw a variety of other "scenic wonders."

It was my first vacation in the U.S. since I started flying, and it was really a pleasant change—no problems with language or money or electricity or airline connections or U. S. Customs. Plus, we were able to eat lots of P's favorite *plat du jour*—hamburgers and French fries.

I'm really looking forward to taking you to Rome and Athens, Mom. Are you positive you won't come with us, Daddy? I have an apartment with a separate bedroom now, so you guys could stay with me on our way "abroad." I'm buying just loads of things for my new pad—hope it's perfect by the time you get here. Even though I'm only on the third floor, the building is a high-rise, so I've named my new apartment Lofty Manor.

Love, Love, Love—
Christine
P.S. I flew with Joan again recently. When I mentioned that I sometimes envision myself pushing P off a cliff, she cautioned, "Don't do it—you might get fired from your job. Besides, I think it may be illegal in the state of New York."

January 30, 1969

My Dear Mary—

Major Conundrum: what to do about Peter. Our plan has been that I fly to Amsterdam to buy the engagement ring next month. But, crazy as I am about the guy, I'm really finding it difficult to commit—for good—to a guy whose sense of reason seems to come and go of its own accord. Plus, there is the more egregious problem of our high-octane arguments, which occur at regular intervals, and consist of P firing the first salvo by berating me for some imaginary thing I've said or done—or failed to say or do—and then my defending myself and shedding buckets of tears, or increasingly often, just feeling wounded and acquiescing, to avoid all the *Sturm und Drang*. As far as I'm concerned, this falls under the heading of police brutality.

My point, which I hope to get to before the end of this letter, is that I guess, like it or not, I will have to break up with my beautiful boy at some point (before blood is spilled), but I'm sure it will be the hardest thing I've ever done. I'm burning up the brain cells trying to figure out what to do and how to do it. You see my dilemma.

Tell me, oh great Oracle, what would you do?

Conflicted—
Chris

February 25, 1969

Hi, Folks—

News Bulletin: Rumors are flying around the airline (pun) that the company is going to open a new International base in Los Angeles for commercial flights to Hong Kong and Bangkok, with layovers in Guam and Honolulu. Pretty heady stuff, huh? And, the best part is that when the company opens a new base, they pay all moving expenses up to 3,000 lbs. of belongings for anyone who transfers there. Sooooo, if I were senior enough to be able to hold that base, it would mean a coast-to-coast move at no cost to me. (I actually got this news straight from the mouth of one of the airline's most respected gossips.)

I've always loved L.A.—it's so relaxed and outdoorsy and un-big-city-like. And, since I moved from there, they have opened the Music Center, with the Dorothy Chandler Pavilion for concerts, and the Ahmanson Theater for plays. The fact that the city is all spread out is a disadvantage, but to be able to fly the Pacific would be a dream gig. And, relocating would provide me with yet another opportunity to pursue what has become my favorite hobby—apartment hunting! I must be the idiot savant of apartment hunting. I could teach Apartment Hunting 101.

In answer to your query about the view from my new Lofty Manor, the answer is yes, I can see the Hudson River— about 2 yards of it.

Love, Love, Love
Christine

February 25, 1969

Dear Mary—

Greetings from Siberia! Yes, I'm still in New York City, but you would never suspect it by the beastly weather we're being subjected to (or, more correctly, to which we are being subjected). Tonight Peter is taking me to Germantown for sauerbraten and then to a movie. Watching TV has been the extent of our whirlwind social life for the last month. We hesitate to venture forth when it's so deadly cold outside that there is the danger of finding ourselves frozen in place within the first five minutes. (Of course, Peter feels the inclement weather has been planned solely to inconvenience Peter.)

My birthday was awful—we were snowed in and couldn't do anything. You, my parents, and Judy were the only ones who remembered it this year. My own personal Blue Period.

Turns out my conundrum concerning P might just work itself out. I may be moving to Los Angeles in a few months to fly the Pacific, in which case the old saying "out of sight—out of mind" would apply, and—*poof*—problem solved. Rather than taking a firm stand, this seems like the easiest way out for a spineless invertebrate like myself.

I suspect you have noticed the only snag in this plan. Yes, I will still be breaking up with P when I tell him I'm moving away. But, how to approach it? Enlighten me, please.

Ciao—
Chris

March 28, 1969

Hi, Mother and Daddy—

Lofty Manor is shaping up nicely—thanks to Bloomingdales' furniture department. I am now the proud owner of a gorgeous new white couch that opens up into a queen-sized bed, and a rosewood dining room table, both of which I will be making payments on - in "small convenient amounts" - for the rest of my life. I had to get a new full-length mirror, too - broke the old one during the move - laid it on the floor and then stepped on it.

Let's plan on the end of April + beginning of May for our jaunt to Rome and Athens, Mom. I just found out my schedule for next month. Suz and I got our first bid (!), so we have three Milan trips and one Athens-Rome-Madrid trip. I get back on April 27, so you and I can leave on our odyssey on the 28th. (I haven't given up on you yet, Daddy.)

I haven't seen Susanne all month—she's on vacation. But, I did have a trip recently with my "bustin' out all over" friend, Joan, and she was in fine form. Of a lady in Coach with wild hair, she said "That's not hair—those are nerve endings." We had a rich, handsome, charming guy on board in First Class, and when he let it drop that he had never been married, Joan turned to me and said, "What diabolical cunning." Later, when he mentioned he couldn't imagine what it would be like to be married, she told him, "Ignorance is no excuse for bliss."

That's our Joan!

Love, Love, Love—
Christine

March 28, 1969

Hi, Mary—

Peter and I went to the Bronx Zoo on Thursday. It's really an old zoo—opened in 1899. Ordinarily, I love zoos. I really do. I enjoy seeing all the different animals and watching them cavort about. But at this sad zoo you can't help feeling sorry for them—the cages are so miserably small they have no room to move around. So they don't. It's disgraceful.

I'm flying to Geneva this month, because it's the only flight we have that stops in Shannon on the way home, so that I can go to the Duty Free shop to buy a camera for Peter to give to his sister for a wedding present. P bought me an exercise bicycle for my birthday—so romantic, huh? We had another industrial-strength argument yesterday—P drove me to the airport, and I cried all the way. I read somewhere recently that crying is good for you, in a way—apparently it has a cleansing effect. But, I've found it also has the side effect of cleansing off all your eye makeup.

Fat lot of good that does.

Ciao—
Chris
P.S. Flew with funny Joan again recently—she professed to be a great fan of George Gershwin—"and his lovely wife, Ira."

April 26, 1969

Dear Mater and Pater –

You may not believe this, but a couple of weeks ago Peter and I went to an off-Broadway play called *The Boys in the Band* and then to dinner, and we actually got through the whole evening without an argument. This must be the way other people live, huh?

I'm glad we decided to change our trip to Athens and Rome to October, Mom, for several reasons, not the least of which is that I filled out the application for the First Class surcharges wrong (or, they didn't understand it), so we wouldn't have had them in time. So, I'll turn the passes back in, and then I will apply for new ones in October.

After I talked to you on the phone on Tuesday, Mom, I went out to the airport and changed our bids for May, because the deadline for bidding wasn't until Wednesday morning. I decided that, instead of having all that time off with nothing specific to do, Suz and I should be making some overtime by flying longer trips. As a result, we got a fantastic bid—one Shannon trip, a Rome trip with a 2-day layover, a Tel Aviv trip, and an Athens trip with a 3-day layover! So, Suz and I will finally get to take that boat trip around the Greek Islands, which we've been wanting to do for eons. Yay!

Love, Love, Love—
Christine

April 26, 1969

Hi, Mary—

I've just had an epiphany! The psychiatrist in me is beginning to suspect that Peter is picking fights with me on purpose—either consciously or subconsciously—because he's tired of me, or for some reason doesn't want to be with me anymore. So that then I will break up with him, and he won't have to break up with me. If so, I hadn't imagined his brain could soar to such lofty heights.

Disaster *du jour*: Tuesday night we went to see a Broadway play called ***Jimmy Shine***—with Dustin Hoffman in the leading role. We had an argument at dinner afterwards, and P said such mean things that I cried all week. (Do you think he must be satisfying some deep, masochistic instinct of mine?) I'm beginning to see the writing on the wall (or is that just graffiti?). After my next trip I have a week off, so I think I'll go down to one of the islands—maybe Aruba or Curacao—just to get away from New York and P for a while and have a good long think about the situation (probably not without thoughts of strangulation).

I'll just bet you're thinking, "For heavens' sake, why doesn't she stop whining and complaining and just break up with the guy?" Good question. I'm glad you thought of it.

Ciao—
Chris

June 2, 1969

Hi, Parents—

What a fun, busy month May was! As you know, I was flying with Susanne. Our first trip of the month was to Shannon, where we kissed the Blarney Stone (again), drank mead, and went to Dromoland Castle, which I have added to my list of magical places in the world. The owner of the castle had erected a statue of a racehorse in the middle of the beautiful gardens, because that was the horse he bet on and won the castle.

As soon as we got home from that trip, we went straight from the airport to Nassau for a few days' vacation. We had a great time there—rode motor scooters all over the island. Our next trip was to Tel Aviv with only a 17-hour layover, so we just had time for a tour of the city, a short swim in the Med and dinner. And so to bed—for a few hours' sleep and then on to Rome. We had a long layover there, so Judy flew over from Munich, and the three of us spent two days together, traipsing all over Rome, seeing all the sights and cackling nonstop.

Our last trip was to Athens with the 3-day layover, so we took a boat tour of Hydra, Delos and Mykonos. The food on the ship was so good that our stomachs won their unequal battle with our brains, and we stuffed to overflowing.

Flew with funny Joan again recently. She stood at the door of the airplane, greeting passengers by saying, "Good morning, sir or madam." And, when she showed a uniformed general to his seat, she said, "Here is your seat, sir—you're 4F." Then, after she made the safety demonstration announcement, she said, "Can you remember all that, boys and girls?"

Gotta flee—
Love, Love, Love—
Christine

June 2, 1969

Hey, Mary—

You will no doubt be relieved to learn (for the simple reason that you won't have to hear any more on the subject) that Peter and I are completely kaput—but still friends. The result on my part is a wonderfully just-slipped-my-leash feeling that makes me want to smile at everyone I see and tell them how happy I am. When I told my funny friend Joan about the breakup, she said, "The handwriting on the wall was as plain as the nose on my face." She told me that she herself is involved in a rather complicated "love trapezoid."

As a parting gift I gave P tickets to the Johnny Carson show that I was going to use with my mom when she was here on our way to Europe, before we changed our plans. So, he's going to use them with his mom. At least, that's what he says.

My mom bought me a chichi new dress, and so far it has been to Shannon, Nassau, Rome, Athens, Tel Aviv and New York and received many admiring glances, which is a very promising kickstart to my entrance back into circulation. I'm beginning to think that my frivolous nature is not conducive to long-term relationships. Or, maybe I'm still in my formative years. Or possibly I'm shallow and self-absorbed. I think it's quite likely that you are tired of all this me, me, me blather and wish I would just shut up. So I will.

Ciao—
Chris

June 30, 1969

Dear M and D—

News Flash! The company is indeed going to open an International base in Los Angeles on August 1 (!!!!!), and being of sound mind and body, I wasted no time at all putting in my request for a transfer. I'm giddy with excitement! I have no idea if I can hold it, but if I can't, I will be sorely disappointed and extremely vexed (isn't that a great word?) and will probably have to be talked down from a window ledge.

I should know in a couple of weeks. This won't affect our trip to Europe, Mom—unless you would rather go to Hong Kong, which is a lot farther, but something to ponder.

Susanne and I have been flying double crossings this month—JFK—LHR—D.C.—FRA—JFK. On our first trip, the D.C. to Frankfurt part cancelled, so they sent us to Paris working a charter, and then we got to deadhead home. In London we saw a play called *In Celebration* with Alan Bates, who (whom?) Suz and I both WORSHIP and ADORE. (Have you seen him in the movie *King of Hearts*? He's brilliant.

In Paris it was too cold to go outside—we shortsightedly took along only summer clothes and no coats. *Quel dommage!* After that we had four days off between trips, so I spent them in Boston with Suz. (Did I tell you she's living there now, commuting to JFK?) We shopped, saw three movies and the Boston Pops. Gotta flee -

Love, Love, Love—
Christine

June 30, 1969

Hi, Mary—

Picture this: It's an unusually warm, sunny day, and Susanne and I are sitting poolside having lunch at our layover hotel in D.C. We're dressed in our best summer frocks, sitting at a table gorging and swilling our lobster salads and raspberry iced teas, surrounded by beautiful people who are ogling other beautiful people and being ogled back. Then, midsentence, I move my chair back a little to get at my purse, when one leg of the chair goes off the edge, tipping it over into the pool, carrying with it an astonished me.

Heads swivel. Forks stop mid air. When I surface, I am mortified to the core to find that I have become the entertainment portion of the afternoon for the delighted beautiful people lunch crowd—who seem unable to stop hooting with laughter. Proving once again that there are endless methods of embarrassing oneself - while throwing off those last pesky little shreds of dignity.

The episode, however, did afford me an introduction to the surprised man who happened to be swimming along and was sent careening across the pool in the seismic aftermath of me and my chair. He made a noise that sounded like "oooargh" and then introduced himself as Rob, who lives in La Jolla. So, if and when I move to L.A., I'll have someone to cavort (or swim) with.

Love,
Chris

July 31, 1969

Hi, Mother and Daddy—

What a whirlwind month this has been! Guess I'll tell you about it in the order things happened. The first week Susanne and I went to Bermuda for a few days between trips—and what a gorgeous island it is. Appropriately, everyone does indeed wear Bermuda shorts and also crash helmets (which come in all colors and designs—plaid, stripes, polka dots, flowers, etc.), because motorbikes are the chosen method of transportation for most people. So, we made like locals and rented motorbikes and donned pink flowered helmets.

When we got back, I found out that my transfer to L.A. had gone through (!), and that all the transferees were to go immediately to Kansas City for two days' Pacific training. When I got back from K.C., I had to hit the ground running to get ready to move to L.A. in three days. Unfortunately, on moving day, the movers didn't come until 7:00 P.M., so I had to leave them in the middle of their packing in order to catch the last flight to L.A., so I would be able to report the next day for a Pacific Orientation talk.

The purpose of the talk, to the extent it appeared to have one, was to inform us that Asians are different from us. Besides the fact that they are shorter (we had to admit we had noticed that) and that they eat all manner of unusual things (we knew that, too), apparently they don't need their "personal space" the way we do. In other words, they don't mind being all crammed together. I took that to mean that they will make ideal passengers.

Love, Love, Love—
Christine

July 31, 1969

Hiya, Mary—

Greetings from L.A.! Yes, my transfer did indeed go through, and I am once again a California girl and looking forward to my new life flying the Pacific. Starting tomorrow I'll be flying to Hong Kong and Bangkok, with layovers in Honolulu and Guam. They are 8-day trips, and we will fly two a month with 7–10 days off between trips. A dream gig, no?

Did you watch the moon landing on TV? I just happened to be in the AA terminal at JFK—had just finished seeing a friend off, when I noticed that everyone in the terminal was glued to a giant TV screen. Talk about serendipity! At that very moment Neil Armstrong stepped onto the surface of the moon, and everyone cheered and hugged each other. What an unforgettable thrill! It brought tears to my eyes.

Tomorrow morning I deadhead to Hong Kong and then work back, with one-day layovers in Guam and Honolulu each way. Then when I get back and come up for air, I will have eight days off (whew!) to once again pursue my favorite hobby—apartment hunting.

Love,
Chris

August 8, 1969

Aloha, Mums and Daddy—

Greetings from Hollywood—land of fruits and nuts. Until my furniture arrives from New York, I'm staying here in Harold's Weekly Apartments (paying $3.75 a night), which, in spite of its unfortunate location in Hollywood, is quite adequate to my needs—for the interim. I found a great apartment in Santa Monica in a perfect location—two blocks from the Miramar Hotel, where the airport limo stops—and three blocks from the beach. The rent is only $165 a month, which includes utilities, and it has a separate bedroom, a garbage disposal and a pool! Interestingly enough, it's only ½ block from where I lived eight years ago. Do you think I'm regressing?

I've had my first trip on the Pacific, and my first without Susanne in several months. Today is her birthday, and I miss her inordinately.

The only dating offers I've had so far were from a 19-year-old, long-haired Canadian kid, who didn't think it was at all funny when I told him I'd go out with him after he finished his homework, and a wizened old bald guy with a well-polished head and eyebrows like two black, fuzzy caterpillars. If he had better posture, he might come all the way up to my clavicle. Also, I suspect he had his shoes on the wrong feet. I am, as you know, just kidding.

Gotta flee—
Love, Love, Love—
Christine

August 8, 1969

Aloha, Mary—

My first trip on the Pacific was uneventful. Hong Kong was hot, Guam was rainy, and Honolulu was perfect. I can tell you here and now that Asian passengers are a delight. They are so quick and so self-sufficient that when they are boarding the airplane, instead of trying to help them, common sense dictates that the best thing to do is to just step back and stay out of their way, lest you be trampled in the onslaught.

My dandy new apartment is one of several that surround a courtyard with a pool, so I've named it Castle Court, as in "a girl's home is her castle." (These names get more pretentious every time I move, huh?) I should be ensconced in it now—this very instant—but Bekins informed me this morning that, for reasons unclear, my furniture is still in New York (!!!). Everyone else's furniture is here except mine. As Peter would say, "Why is it always me?"

I have no friends here except the people I fly with, thus I find myself home alone on a Friday night, feeling abandoned by a cruel, uncaring world. I think I'll go curl up with a good book. I might even read it.

Love,
Chris

September 1, 1969

Hi, Mums and Daddy –

My tardy furniture finally put in an appearance last week, so I've spent the last few days feathering my new nest. The furniture arrived relatively unscathed, although my rosewood end table is sporting some big ugly scratches, and the couch is torn here and there—and a clock is missing. The driver of the delivery truck says that the Claims Department will "fix it" for me, so I immediately put in a call to them, and they're going to send someone over "one of these days."

I should be applying for the passes pretty soon for our trip, Mums, so—difficult as I know it is for you—we really should make up our minds where we want to go. Makes no difference to me. I'll bid to have at least the last week of October and the first week of November off, so I guess we know the "when," and now we must put our brains in gear and figure out the "where." To answer your questions: yes, all of my passes can be used overseas now (it used to be only two). And, next year I get 8 passes instead of 6—and 3 weeks' vacation instead of 2. Yes, we could fly around the world. It would cost $63 each ($113 for First Class). Do you want to? Where "in the world" shall we go?

Adventure beckons!

Love, Love, Love—
Christine

September 1, 1969

Aloha, Mary—

I'm sitting in Castle Court, looking at my newly arrived furniture, bemoaning the fact that the place is carpeted, and the manager won't let me put my big, beautiful red shag rug down over it, so that my whole color scheme (red and black) is ruined, because their carpeting is light green. *Merde*!!

So far I've gone out with two guys here in L.A., both deeply flawed. One was a real knuckle dragger - his neck was wider than his head—a best-kept-well-hidden sort of person. The other one was a more highly evolved organism, but when he spoke, it sounded as if he could do with a chest X-ray, and his hairline appeared to be in full retreat. Spartan fare.

BUT! Remember Rob—the man I swamped in the pool in D.C. a couple of months ago? I spent last weekend in La Jolla visiting him—had a great time—went to the beach and to the zoo. He's a little younger than I am (I call him Babycakes), and a little too tall (6'4") and divorced, but he's really a very nice guy—very gentle and soft spoken - and relentlessly clever. I may just be in love again—sort of.

I'm off to Honolulu in a few hours. It looks as though I'm going to have to bid as much overtime as I can in order to buy all the myriad things Hong Kong has to offer, like watches, jewelry, cameras, hi-fi equipment, designer sunglasses, silk fabric, clothes made to order and on and on. I'm hooked!

Love,
Chris

October 4, 1969

Hi, Mums and Daddy—

Since I haven't been in trouble with the company for a long while, the fact that I missed a flight recently didn't get me in very much hot water—not as much as missing a flight normally would. (By that, I mean that I wasn't flogged or stoned to death.) Here's what happened: Unbeknownst to me, the flight times for the month were posted in Greenwich Mean Time, whereas I was operating on local time, like we did in New York. I guess the reason for that is that we go through so many time zones on our way to Hong Kong or Bangkok that the whole trip is listed in GMT, and you have to figure it out for yourself. Turns out I was actually supposed to report the day before I thought I was. Anyhow, they didn't take me off schedule or anything, which would have meant losing $. They just put me on the same flight two days later. A little snag in the otherwise smooth fabric of my life.

I put in for the passes for our trip, Mums. I plan to meet you in Chicago on the way over, because there is a Chicago—Rome flight daily. It stops in Paris, but if we got bumped in Paris, it wouldn't break our hearts, huh? Let's go First Class. The flights are pretty long, especially coming back from Athens—New York, which is about 10 hours. It only costs $16. OK? OK!

Love, Love, Love—
Yer Dum Daughter—Christine

October 4, 1969

Hi, Mary—

Rob (Babycakes) surprised me and met my flight Sunday night, and I surprised him by having on my new curly blond wig. I got it in Honolulu, and it's the answer to all my hair problems, caused by wind, rain, humidity (also, possible hurricanes, typhoons, volcanic eruptions—ha ha) in the Pacific.

We're having a great time together (Rob and I—not my wig and I). He spent a weekend in Santa Monica, and then I went to La Jolla, and we drove down to Mexico in his little sports car. I would have sent you a postcard, but we were in a tiny fishing village called San Felipe, where they didn't even have such a luxury as a post card. He called me on the phone last night and told me he's "serious" about me. Be still my heart!

My well-endowed friend Joan is flying the Pacific, too, now, and I had a trip with her recently. At one point the call button rang in 12C, and she asked me if I wanted to answer it because the guy in that seat was "a splendid-looking specimen." I've decided she's the Tom Sawyer of hostesses. Later on, someone asked her if she ever got hungry in the middle of the night, and she said, "How do I know? I'm sound asleep."

The purser told me that the first officer asked her out, and she told him, "I've divorced better men than you."

Love,
Chris

November 28, 1969

Hi, Folks—

Did you receive the pictures I took on our trip, Mums? They are for you to keep. I had another set made for myself. To answer the four questions from your last letter: The food we liked so much in Rome is called Canneloni (yum). And, the restaurant where we ate the roast pig is called De Meo Patacca (yum, again). Yes, Bekins fixed the scratches on my end table so it looks just like new, and they also sewed up the holes in the couch, so you can't even see where they were. So, just like the delivery man assured me, they "fixed it" for me. And, yes, Mums, we get only one winter uniform. I could have a second one in a different color, but I would have to pay for it myself. Besides, I think both Pea green and Halloween orange are hideously unflattering colors. I'll stick with my yellow.

I'm holding a great schedule for December. I fly only one 6-day trip, out the 18th and back the 25th. I consider myself lucky to hold that bid—only 10 girls in the whole base got both Christmas and New Years' off, and I'm # 33 in seniority. So, at least I have Christmas night and New Years to spend with Rob.

I have two passes left for 1969, to be used before March 15, and I need to apply for them before December 31. We have a nonstop from ORD to LHR, Mums, if you want to go there for a few days and see some plays. Ponder that.

Love, Love, Love—
Christine

November 28, 1969

Hi, Mary—

Had a better-than-average Thanksgiving this year. Spent it with Babycakes — just the two of us. I tempted fate once again by venturing back into my personal hellhole known as … the kitchen. This time I went all out with the comestibles and made the usual suspects—turkey, dressing, yams, gravy, cranberries, creamed onions and pumpkin pie—most of which were actually quite edible. A chef I'm not, but I appear to be improving decidedly. Albeit, gradually.

Then, when I went to the airport that night for my flight, I had another instance of Peter's, "Why is it always me?" While I was upstairs in the hanger checking in, I left my suitcase and airline bag on the luggage rack in the lobby (everyone does), and someone stole out of my airline bag - of all things—my new wig! My insurance will cover it, but now I have to buy another wig, report the theft to the police, and file a claim.

Don't you just hate it when life gets in the way of your fun?

Ciao—
Chris
P.S. Flew with funny Joan again recently. One of the passengers was asking her how to work the Inflight Entertainment system, so she said, "If you figure out how it works, please let us know."

December 25, 1969

Merry Christmas, dear Parents—

Just got in from Honolulu, and I'm waiting at the airport for the bus to Santa Monica. This has really been a goofy Christmas. First of all, we celebrated Christmas Eve in Guam and then took off from there about 2 A.M. on Christmas day—flew east for about three hours, crossed the International Date Line, and then it was Christmas Eve again, which we celebrated in Honolulu. That was yesterday. Now today I'm having another Christmas. (I haven't enjoyed either of them that much.) Most of our passengers were seasoned travelers, by which I mean drunk.

I had originally planned to spend today with Rob, but since I last wrote to you, he broke up with me. We hadn't seen each other long enough for there to be any permanent damage, but still I was in sort of a funk for a couple of weeks. Guess I'll look back on that as my own personal Blue Period (another one).

Susanne has been here several times this month on layovers (she's flying Domestic now, out of Boston). She makes an excellent grief counsellor. She's coming in day after tomorrow on another layover, and I plan to go back to Boston with her the next day and spend New Year's Eve with her. She doesn't have a date, either. Works out well when we are both "between men" at the same time.

The bus just drove up—gotta bounce—

Love, Love, Love—
Christine

December 25, 1969

Mele Kalikimaka, Mary—

As you may have surmised, that is Hawaiian for Merry Christmas.

    I'll go straight to the point and evade all side issues. Babycakes broke up with me! Extremely hurtful! ("He jests at scars who never felt a wound.") The fact that he was too tall and too young is scant comfort. I did as Helen Gurley Brown advised in *Sex and the Single Girl*—had a good cathartic cry over what might have been and moved on. End of Rob era.

    Ironically enough, my new beau, a German named Boris, is even younger. But, he is SUCH a handsome creature, in a blond, tanned, Aryan sort of way. I call him "Goldilocks." He's a real hunk. Although, it's pretty difficult to have a meaningful dialogue with such a strong, overly-silent type of hunk. He's the opposite of outgoing. Would that be incoming?

    One weekend we played volleyball on the beach two days in a row with a bunch of his German friends. (I've been sore all over ever since.) On Saturday night we went to the movies, and Sunday night we drank beer and played darts with his friends at a local English pub. It was the most fun weekend I've had in eons.

    He said he would meet my flight tonight if he didn't go skiing, but he didn't, so I guess he did.

Love,
Chris

January 31, 1970

Hi, Folks

It just occurred to me that if I bid to fly to Hong Kong on Feb 9, and lay over in Honolulu on the 10th, so that I cross the International Date Line and skip the 11th altogether, I won't have to have a birthday. And, if I do that every year, I can stay the same age indefinitely! Brilliant, huh?

Yes, I'm dieting again, Mom. Guess I have finally come to realize that dieting is going to have to be a lifetime effort if I want to avoid having a body that takes up more space than it should. That's my excuse for ordering champagne instead of beer these days—it's less fattening. My first week on my current diet showed some change, but not much—I gained 3 lbs.

Yes, Daddy, I've been reading some good books. Lately I've read **Oliver Twist** - then **Far From the Madding Crowd** – then **The Grapes of Wrath**, and now I'm into **The First Circle**, which I'm especially enjoying. Russian authors have always been my favs.

And now for the Problem du Jour, which concerns my hair. On a recent layover I ventured into the salon in the Hong Kong Hilton for a touchup, and much to my surprise, I walked out a redhead! There was no time to remedy it there, so when I got to Honolulu, I went to Elizabeth Arden for reparation and was surprised again when they turned the red into a muddy shade of brown! They kept insisting it was blond, so I cried a lot, and they didn't make me pay for it, which was scant comfort.

Hope I haven't abused your patience with the preceding vanity. I imagine most people in the world would wish their problems were that trivial, huh?

That's all she wrote –
Christine

January 31, 1970

Hau'oli Makahiki Hoa, Mary—

That means Happy New Year in Hawaiian, in case you had any doubt.

In re my blond beau Boris (aka Goldilocks): He called two days after Christmas and said he was there at the airport on Christmas night to meet my flight, but he was late, and I had left already. (Did I believe that? Maybe.) Then he asked me to go skiing that weekend with him and his friends if there was snow, and said that he was having a New Year's Eve party if they didn't go skiing. But, he never called back to tell me if there was snow. I didn't want to wait around for him to call and then, if he didn't, not have anything to do on New Year's Eve, so I went back to my original plan and went to Boston to revel with Suzanne. An unimpeachable source (a friend of mine who went to his party) told me they had 30 bottles of champagne, and Boris didn't have a date—he was by himself.

Meanwhile, Suz and I went to a party in Boston, which turned out to be *tres jolie*. I was the only one there with a suntan, and I wore a white dress, so I didn't go unnoticed.

I'm going to visit Judy in Munich next month before her 5-year stint is up and the State Department sends her to her next gig. On the way, I'm going to Houston to visit a pilot I met on my last flight. If he turns out to be a major player, I'll elaborate in my next letter.

Watch this space.

Aloha (until we meet again) -
Chris

February 15, 1970

Guten Tag, Folks—

Enclosed is a post card that I meant to send you from Munich, but I left in such a mad dash that I forgot to mail it. It was, of course, great to see Judy again, but she had to work during the day, so I mostly shopped for more Rosenthal china and for something to wear to a costume ball for Fasching, which is their pre-Lenten celebration—sort of like Mardi Gras, I guess. She fixed me up with a friend of her boyfriend—we had a pretty good time—drank champagne 'til dawn. When they make up their minds to have fun, no one does it better than the Germans.

Judy's job entails interviewing Germans to determine if they get a visa to go to the U.S.—all transacted in German. Now, although she took German in college and, I guess, a refresher course before she moved there, she didn't imagine it would be so difficult. Apparently they speak "low" German there in Munich, while the German she learned was "high" German.

Munich is a lovely city, and she has a pretty nifty setup—a two-bedroom, rent-free apartment, one block from the Consulate where she works, PX privileges, an office of her own with a secretary, an English sports car - plus a gorgeous blond boyfriend - so that she hates to leave, but her tour is up. And, so is this letter.

Love, Love, Love—
Christine

February 15, 1970

Aloha, Mary—

Must hasten to tell you about my new flavor of the month. His name is Ted—a first officer for TWA—32—divorced—6"2'—and is soooo ripe for picking. He commutes to New York from Houston, where he has a new 4-bedroom house, a boat, 3 cars, 3 airplanes, and best of all, he's ultramasculine—makes the guys I've gone with lately seem like mere boys. We had such a good time when I stopped to see him on my way to Munich, that I stopped again for a few days on my way home. I met a lot of his friends, and he took me flying in his biplane.

Speaking of flying, on my last layover in Honolulu, another girl and I were all set to go to the beach, when we met a captain from Pan Am on the hotel elevator, who invited us to go soaring with him up on the north shore of the island, so of course we jumped at the chance. It was really a kick. You get into this little plane with no engine - called a glider—pilot in front, us behind, and a truck pulls you along until you catch the wind current, which takes you up in the air. (The driver of the truck told us to "have a good flight and try not to die.") Evidently the winds are particularly good in that area—also the surf—because they come all the way across the Pacific Ocean with nothing to stop them. Makes sense, huh? Anyhow, it was really neat up there—all quiet and beautiful. And super thrilling.

Love,
Chris

March 21, 1970

Hi, Mums and Daddy—

News Bulletin from the front: TWA has a terrific new pass policy. We each get an extra pass for ourselves and 2 extra passes for our parents (or, husband, or children), that are above and beyond the 8 passes a year we already get—as long as they are used during our vacation period. My vacation this year is October 17—November 8. I haven't decided yet where to go, except that I'll have a lot (for me) of $ saved by then, so I'd like to make it a big one. If you would like to go to Germany together, we could do that, or if you two would like to use your two passes to go somewhere else, then I would go to Asia or India or somewhere really exotic.

The neatest thing happened to me this week—a TWA lawyer called me from New York and asked if I would come there to testify at a trial concerning an incident that happened on one of my flights five years ago. As a result, I got a Pay Assignment, which means I get taken off a flight and paid for it, but I don't have to go on it. So, tomorrow I'm going to New York on the 747, which is the big, new jumbo jet, which I haven't been on yet. (We fly the smaller 707 on the Pacific.) I've never been part of a trial before—or even been in a courtroom.

Well, this is my 10th day off, and true to form, I've gotten almost nothing done, so I have to do everything all in one day—today.

Love, Love, Love—
Christine

March 21, 1970

Yo, Mary—

Ted, my flavor of the month, turned out to be just that. A couple of weeks ago he met my flight—turned up wearing a tie of considerable ugliness - with little airplanes all over it! Very telling, don't you think? Besides our divergent tastes in neckwear, I've found that we really have no significant mutual interests. For instance, he confesses that the only reading he does is from the menu at the Crab Shack. Compared to him, I'm one of the great thinkers of all time. I rest my case.

The other day I flew with a really funny girl whose name is Jan. We had a baby on board who cried nonstop for the whole flight. We also had a young couple on board who complained about the crying baby—nonstop for the whole flight. After we landed, and the couple was deplaning, Jan asked them if they had any children yet. They answered no, they didn't. So, Jan said to them, "Well, don't!"

My old beau Alistair from New York has been in touch—tells me he has letters of introduction to some people at a 12th century French chateau in Burgundy to taste some vintage wines (which I wouldn't know from Gallo Hearty Burgundy). He also said we could go to Bayreuth to see Wagner's estate—I'm a big Wagner fan (of his music, not of the arrogant genius himself). And, also, I've had a few dates with the mayor of L.A.'s press secretary, so—adventure beckons!

Love,
Chris

April 4, 1970

Hi, Folks—

Unfortunately, my trip to New York City for the trial was not without incident. I left on Easter Sunday on the 747 jumbo jet (amidst a cast of thousands), and all was routine until we went to land at JFK, where it had been snowing, so the airport closed, and we were diverted to Washing, D.C., where the flight canceled! So, we were forced to abandon the mother ship and were then sent to JFK on busses (all 312 of us), which took 7 gruesome hours. We arrived all bleary eyed and grumbly at 4:00 A.M. and were told that we would have our luggage by 8:00 A.M.—I finally got mine at 1:30 P.M., but only because I chased it down.

The trial started on Tuesday—I testified on Thursday, and the verdict on Friday was in TWA's favor. We won! Thereby saving the company a whopping $22,500. My first time in a courtroom was an eye-opening experience. Two things seemed obvious to me. The first was that people under oath tell the truth. The second, also wrong, was that the accuser's lawyer is impartial. Turns out the accuser's lawyer was her uncle. The judge didn't seem to like that.

I came home yesterday—again on a 747—again amidst a full load of snarling passengers, but this time it was because we were 4 hours late and because the movie broke down. Consequently, I've taken a firm stand, and it is definitely anti-747. From the time you stand in line for several years to check in and board the behemoth (which is as big as greater Detroit) until the time you hang around the baggage claim area for several more years for your luggage, you've encountered and interacted with half the population of the Western world.

Traveling with large assemblages is not my cup of *the* (French word for "tea").

Love, Love, Love—
Christine

April 4, 1970

Yo, Mary—

Zounds! Looks as though I won't be meeting Alistair in Europe after all—his business meeting is at the end of May, but I can't use my International passes after May 15, so that's that.

I broke up with Ted on the phone last week, and it didn't bother me a bit. In fact, I've hardly thought about him since. Goodbye flyboy!

I'm currently on a very strict diet. I've lost 6-8 lbs. so far and will stay the course until people look at me and say, "Oh my, she's so painfully thin!" I found some mild appetite suppressant pills in Hong Kong that I can get without a prescription, so that makes it easier, although as I write this I feel like I haven't eaten since early childhood.

I got in a little bit of trouble the other day—while we were waiting for catering to board the food, I was overheard saying, "Let them eat cake," so I was called into the office and duly chastised. Apparently, it is a punishable offense.

Ciao—
Chris
P.S. It's spring! When a young woman's fancy lightly turns to thoughts of new clothes.

May 6, 1970

Hi, Folks—

I've just concluded a most pleasant 9 days off, pursuing my current favorite hobby—get ready for this—cooking! At this point I think I have definitely turned the corner in my relentless pursuit of adequacy in the kitchen. Did I tell you that I bought a copy of **Helen Gurley Brown's Single Girl's Cookbook,** and as a result I have made a few dishes that would definitely not fall into the "crime against nature" category of my earlier efforts? I'm doing my very best to avoid concocting any more burnt offerings.

Also, among the flotsam and jetsam known as my belongings, I came across a copy of **The Good Housekeeping International Cookbook,** which must have been accompanying me in my various moves for several years, so I finally cracked it open and found a few gems, among the best of which are an Australian beef and veg casserole, a Yugoslavian dish called Djuvetsch and a lemon tortoni.

This week I've been breakfasting on pancakes with cloves, cinnamon and nutmeg in the batter - with strawberry syrup on top. Yum! (Excuse me while I wipe the saliva off my chin.) Predictably, though, after tucking away all those pancakes, I gained back a lb. this week. *Merde!*

Love, Love, Love—
Christine

May 31, 1970

Hi, Mary—

Do you remember Dick, who was my old boss that I was so wild about when I was working my way through college? Well, he's going through a divorce now and living in New York.

We've always kept in touch and gotten together from time to time, so at his invitation I went to see him last week, and we had the BEST time. He met me at the airport and went with me to my annual check-up with the boob doctor (who had removed the lump from my breast a few years ago), and that night we (Dick and I—not the doc and I) went to a cute Italian restaurant in G. Village. The next night we saw a play called **Child's Play**, which has won 4 Tonys. The next day was gorgeous, so we walked in Central Park, and in the afternoon we went to a play called **Promises, Promises**, then to New Jersey to visit some friends of Dick's. The next day I visited Katy for a while, and then we (Dick and I—not Katy and I) went to Radio City to see the movie **Airport** and then had dinner at his fav bar on the East Side, where we ran into some of his friends. It was the most fun I've had in eons, as a result of which I want you to be the first to know that we're going to get married (yes, dear, to each other).

The only major drawback is that he has accepted a job in Decatur, Illinois (!)—not exactly on everyone's list of never-to-be-missed cities of the world. So, I plan to commute to either LAX or JFK and keep flying (my motto) until I'm so old I'll be serving those meals from a wheelchair and doing the emergency demo while drooling on the life vest.

Ciao –
Chris

June 24, 1970

Hi, Parents—

So nice to hear your voice on the phone, Mom. I won't leap
to Dick's defense, because what you feel about him may well
be true, however, I have encountered plenty of playboys, and
I wouldn't put Dick in that category. I want you to know
that I have not ventured into the field of engagement lightly.
(That was a pun, like it or not.)

Apropos of nothing, I flew with a very senior girl the
other day whose name is Jean Bone, and she was reminiscing
about her first trip as a hostess years ago. She was on a Martin
airplane, which has just one hostess, so she was flying solo, so
to speak, and she was, of course, a nervous wreck. When she
made her announcement welcoming the passengers on board,
she was supposed to introduce the two pilots in the cockpit
and end her speech with "and, I am your hostess Miss Bone."
Instead she was horrified to hear herself say, "and, I am your
bone, Miss Hostess."

Guess I'd better go study a little—our Annual Emergency
Review is tomorrow, and we have to make 90%, or get taken
off the payroll until we do. My manual beckons -

Love, Love, Love—
Christine
P.S. Had my hair done in Hong Kong last trip, and the girl
said to me, "I sink your hair is pity fruffy."

June 24, 1970

Aloha, Mary—

News Flash: Dick called last night to say that he is now divorced—no waiting time—it's final right now. (He also said that it cost him 2 arms and 2 legs.) I'm definitely not going to rush into anything, though. Turns out it would be too expensive for me to commute from Decatur to LAX to fly the Pacific, so I want to stay here and fly these flights (which I LOVE—each one is like a vacation) for at least a year. Since I'm not exactly engaged—with a ring (a small, but real distinction), I've decided to keep my options open until I've actually plighted my troth. (When I asked him— jokingly - if he was going to buy me a ring, he looked at me like I had invented the word.)

Which will explain the following: I went to a vascular surgeon last week for the varicose vein in my leg, for which said surgeon gave me an injection to collapse said vein. "He" is young, tall, and darkly handsome, and he gave me a ride home (in his snazzy Cadillac convertible), and we have a date for lunch next week. "Lunch," rather than dinner—meaning that he could well be married. We'll see.

Yes, I have read *Tai Pan*—really enjoyed it. The fact that I'm in Hong Kong twice a month made it especially relevant.

Ta Ta—
Chris
P.S. It just occurred to me that we got through what I understand is now called the "Swinging 60's" without becoming an addict, getting pregnant, or getting arrested. Whew!

July 20, 1970

Hi, Folks—

Did I tell you that the lease on Castle Court is up at the end of the month? (Where did the last year go? Must be some sort of a time warp going on here.) As you know, I'm no stranger to apartment hunting, so before my last trip, I resumed my perennial hobby, although this time I was hampered by the fact that my expense check, which would have served as my deposit, had gone missing. So, after being bounced back and forth several times between the unhelpful-and-uncaring woman at the company payroll office and the unhelpful-and-uncaring woman at the bank, my check finally surfaced—in someone else's bank account. I find it very disturbing when the bank errs—one likes to picture one's $ safely tucked away in some huge, impenetrable bank vault.

Anyhow, I got lucky apartment-wise. As of August 1 I will be living a whole block away from where I live now. The new apartment is pretty spiffy—has a private balcony, a fireplace, dishwasher and a buzzer system to let people in—like we had in New York. (You sure do get a whole lot more bang for your buck here in L.A. than you do in New York.) It's on the second floor, so I've named it Castle Tower. My doctor friend offered to help me move, but only half-heartedly, so I declined—but I did accept the offer to use his car.

My last trip was just about the best ever. The whole crew is insanely fun—we laugh incessantly - like a pack of hyenas. The weather was gorgeous everywhere, and we moved to a plush new layover hotel in Guam. (Yes, there is such a thing as a plush hotel in Guam.) What a way to earn the 3 squares, huh?

Love, Love, Love—
Christine

July 20, 1970

Yo, Mary—

The 4ᵗʰ of July this year fell on a Saturday—a beautiful, sunny day—so I joined 9/10 of the population of Los Angeles at the beach. Satan also put in an appearance that afternoon at the beach—in the form of a carbon copy of Peter—just as good looking—bright—clever—very sweet—great bod— no future. But, you will be relieved to hear that I did not bite into that apple this time. Once bitten, twice shy. (Those two clichés don't quite work together, but you know what I mean, huh?)

Dick and I had an okay time while he was here. I think the most memorable thing about his visit was the afternoon/ evening we spent in Pasadena at the 100ᵗʰ birthday party for Dick's grandfather's sister. She is quite alert—told me that Dick's ancestors came from Schleswig-Holstein and that his father was president of the Tri-City Symphony for a while. What an inspiration she is! I've already started planning my 100ᵗʰ birthday party—I'm going to serve loads of champagne—will you come? I think you'll be about 98.

Flew with funny Joan again—at one point in the flight someone asked her, "How many hostesses work on this flight?" To which she replied, "About half of them."

Ciao—
Chris

August 31, 1970

Hi, Mom and Dad—

Made a new friend this month, and it turns out that we have the same vacation time this year, so we're thinking of going to the USSR together. It won't be the same trip I did before—we want to take the Trans-Siberian Railroad from Vladivostok, which is on the east coast of the USSR, all the way across to Moscow, with a couple of stops on the way. Then we'll go up to Leningrad for a few days and down to Kiev for a few more days. We'll have the last two weeks of October and the first two weeks of November to do all that. Yes, I know it will be zero cold there at that time, but that's the best vacation bid we could hold.

My new friend's name is Josie, and she's very funny and witty, in a quiet sort of way. We were having breakfast the other day in Guam, and the menu listed eggs prepared "as you like them." So, when the waitress came to take her order, Josie told her that she would have eggs "as I like them." And, one time when we were having dinner in Honolulu, she kept asking the waiter what was included with each entrée, so when the check came, she said, "Is that included with the meal?" And once when describing her aunt, she said, "She has the kind of face that people say that she has a great personality."

She makes me laugh, and she laughs at my jokes, so what more could you ask for in a friend?

Love, Love, Love—
Christine

August 31, 1970

Hi, Mary—

I'm having a rather uneventful week off between trips.
Although, one night I did go to the opening of a swanky new
hotel in San Diego with the mayor's press secretary. We ate
a big, fancy dinner, drank champagne and danced to Freddy
Martin. Yeah, yeah, I know I've always been a real clod on
the dance floor, but now after a few inhibition-liberating
glasses of champagne, I can get up there and sort of "wing
it." And, if I look like a booby, so be it.

In answer to your query about movie stars/prominent
personages on our Pacific flights, yes, we have had a few on
flight. Not nearly as many as on the flights from New York to
Europe, of course, but I have had Don Ho, Burgess Meredith
and Kris Kristofferson on board. And, James Mason and
I smiled at each other in the lobby of the Hong Kong Hilton.

Yes, dearie, I do fly both to Bangkok and Hong Kong—
not in the same trip, though. They are two different trips,
so we bid either/or. And, yes, while I really enjoy Bangkok,
there will always be a special place in my heart for Hong
Kong. It's such a treat to go there twice a month. I admire
the Chinese immensely—they are so energetic and hard
working. I find their whole culture—what I've learned about
it—just fascinating. So different from ours. Flying there is the
ultimate of dream gigs.

Love —
Chris

September 29, 1970

Hi, Parents—

I got a strike ballot in the mail today. Even though it could very well bugger up our vacation plans, I voted to go on strike. I decided that one has to take a wider view and do what is right for the majority. (Do I sound like a Bolshevik?) I feel a finer person now. Ha ha

Josie and I went downtown Los Angeles today to the Intourist office and made all the arrangements for our trip to the USSR next month. We'll be gone a month, but we won't spend more than 3 nights in any one place. Our itinerary goes thusly: We leave October 19 on TWA (or Pan Am if we're on strike) and go to Taipei for a couple of days—then take Japan Airlines to Tokyo and overnight there—then a train to Yokohama—then a 52-hour boat ride to Khabarovsk – then a train to Vladivostok, where the Trans-Siberian Railroad begins. Then its 3 days on the train to Irkutsk—2 days there—2 days on the train to Novosibirsk—2 days there—and 2 days on the train to Moscow. We arrive on November 7, which is their winning of the Bolshevik revolution celebration. We stay there 3 days—fly to Kiev and stay there for 2 days— fly to Leningrad and stay there 3 days. On November 16 we fly to Helsinki—overnight there, and the next day, if we make all our connections, we'll take Finnair to Frankfurt and TWA to NYC and L.A.

Around the world in 30 days!

Love, Love, Love—
Christine

September 29, 1970

Dear Mary—

I'm off to the USSR again next month on vacation. I'm going with a different girl this time, and we're taking the Trans-Siberian Railroad across the country, so it should be a real kick.

One of the places we stop is Irkutsk, where we are told that the mean temperature is 0 degrees! So, I plan to buy long thermal underwear and warm boots and to take the big fur hat I bought there last time. When it comes to warmth versus looks, I haven't the remotest acquaintance with vanity.

I think Irkutsk must be one of the coldest cities in the world. The Russians (Soviets, they call themselves) seem to have the "est" of everything in the world—the deepest lake (Baikal), the best ballet corps, the longest railway, the biggest wooly mammoth skeleton, etc. etc. But, who are we to argue?

Packing for this trip is going to be a challenge—we'll be gone a month, so we have to take lots and lots of warm, heavy clothing. I'm going to buy a new suitcase—I'll be looking for one that's big on the inside and small on the outside. If that ever gets invented, be sure to let me know. Would I buy one? You betcha!

Das Vidana—
Chris

10/23/70—here in Tokyo
10/22/70 in the U.S.

Hi, Folks—

I got as far as Guam on TWA before the strike began. Whew! But, yesterday, when I went to check in for the Pan Am flight to Tokyo, they wouldn't let me on the flight (!) because I didn't have a visa for Japan. They were adamant, despite my nonsensical protestations that Intourist told us we didn't need one if we were staying less than 72 hours, which turns out to be true, provided you leave Japan from the same point from which you entered. But, since we are flying to Tokyo and sailing out of Yokohama, they do require a visa. (A visa! A visa! My kingdom for a visa!) So, I went back to the hotel in Guam, feeling alienated by a cruel, uncaring world, and had a good sobfest, convinced my vacation had been totally ruined.

I suspect you will find it hard to believe this part—I scarcely do myself. The stars must have been aligned just right, because the following day (today), with a lot of help from the Japan Airlines ticketing people (and doubtless some Divine intervention), I was able to get on a plane to Okinawa, get a visa there, and get on another plane to Tokyo—all in the same day! I assume it was a miracle, for no other reason than it was.

I'm only a day late to Tokyo, so today I went over to the local Intourist office to pick up the documents for the rest of the trip. After that scare, I feel the powers that be owe me a seamless trip from here on out.

Love, Love, Love—
Christine

10/23/70—here in Tokyo
10/22/70 in the U.S.

Hi, Mary—

As it happened (and with a little planning) Susanne was traveling on the same flight I took from L.A. to Guam on the first leg of my vacation to the USSR. She was on her way to the Philippines to visit a foster child she sponsors there. She was traveling in First Class on a pass, so the purser moved me up from Coach so that I could sit next to her. We had THE BEST flight ever—feasting on chateaubriand and champagne and talking nonstop all the way.

A couple of days before I left on this trip, Josie, the girl I'm taking the trip with, developed some sort of physical problem, so she couldn't leave with me, but she said that if she got it taken care of in the next couple of days, she would catch up with me in Tokyo. Neither of us had a hotel lined up here, so I don't know how we'll hook up. I'm just doing the trip as planned and fervently hope she turns up at some point. I'm not worried about doing the trip alone, but I know that two heads are better than one when it comes to having fun, and you are well aware of my lifelong preference for fun over—well, anything else!

Das Vidanyah—
Chris

November 23, 1970

Dear *Maht and Ah-tetz*—(phonetically, Russian for mother and daddy)

Do you have my postcard from the USSR yet? Probably not, but when you do, you'll notice that the four big stamps cover almost the whole card, so my message was—of necessity—succinct.

The vacation went off smoothly enough but pretty much as I expected—not a whole lot of fun, but an unforgettable experience, nevertheless. We did lots of sightseeing on the trip, some of which I'd done before. We had five days in Moscow this time, and we got to see three ballets at the Bolshoi and also the Moscow Circus. We had three days in Leningrad—saw a ballet and an opera there, then flew to Kiev, which is a pretty city on a hill—had two days there and saw another opera. If we hadn't known from our concierge at the hotel what performance we were buying tickets for—and hadn't been familiar with the music - we wouldn't have had a clue what we were seeing, because they don't print programs, and nobody speaks English. So unfortunately, we'll never know the names of the performers - who were extraordinary.

The Trans Siberian Railroad part of the trip was a never-to-be-forgotten experience. The train schedule runs on Moscow time the whole way, even though we crossed nine time zones. So, we never knew what time of day - or night—it was, wherever we were. And, meals were served in the dining car at the oddest times—like, just as we had planned to go to bed—or in the middle of the night—or in the middle of what seemed to be afternoon. And, we couldn't actually tell what meal it was meant to be—there was a lot of beef Stroganoff sort of thing—some bare pancakes that might have been crepes—and some sandwiches with what seemed to be meat in there. All quite tasty, however.

Our most precious traveling companion turned out to be my old friend the Berlitz Phrase book—the same one I used five years ago with Susanne. Once you learn the alphabet, it opens up a whole new world. When you sound out the words, some of them actually sound like the English equivalent. For instance, *pectopah* actually sounds sort of like "restaurant."

You may have heard our strike lasted only three days, so now we have a new contract. We've been working under our old, expired contract for 15 months. We got a salary increase of 13%, so I should get so much retroactive pay that I will have to hire an armored car to get it to the bank. Ha ha.

Das Vidanya –
Christine

November 24, 1970

Dobray-ootroh, Comrade Mary –

Well, Josie did catch up with me in Tokyo. In fact, we ran into each other quite by accident in the lobby of the hotel that, unbeknownst to either of us, we were both staying in. So, we trotted right over to the Intourist office to get our vouchers, took the train to Kamakura, and from there a ship to Nakhodka, then a train to Vladivostock, where the Trans Siberian Railroad actually starts (or ends, depending, of course, on which end you're looking at it from).

We spent three days in Irkutsk (a big yawn except for the circus and Lake Baikal) because our subsequent stop in Novosibersk was - for reasons unknown—cancelled. Intourist moves in mysterious ways, its miracles to perform.

The train trip was an unforgettable experience. We were put in a compartment with four berths—two up and two down—two of which we had to share with whomever happened to get on the train at one of the countless stops we made. For a time we even had to share with two Russian guys. No problem there, though—they stayed on their side of the compartment, we on ours. And, the next day we had fun trying to communicate with each other (with the help of some vodka they provided) via hand gestures and snippets of felonious English and Russian, gleaned on our part from our precious Berlitz Russian phrase book.

At the back of each of the cars was a female attendant, who oversaw an enormous samovar, so we were provided with endless cups (glasses, actually) of hot, flavorful tea - they call it Chai. We loved our lady—she was an act of God. She was sort of a rugged light heavyweight with a longish black mustache. She made sure to let us know when food was being served in what was laughingly called the dining room, which was a smoke-filled car (Russians smoke incessantly— even when they're eating) with wooden picnic tables and benches, full of drunken, shouting, ogling men. We didn't know what or how to order, so we just sat and waited until someone brought us something that looked like actual food, which turned out to taste just fine.

The romantic Russian countryside I had dreamed of proved disappointing. It was mile after mile after unrelenting mile of birch trees, birch trees, and more boring birch trees. Apparently, we were asleep when we went over the Urals, worst luck.

The weather couldn't have been worse—zero cold, of course, and it snowed incessantly and then melted into dirty slush or water-on-top-of-ice. What else could we expect in November, you might well ask. I'm really not complaining. We got a taste of the famous Russian winter that we'll never forget.

But, at the same time, I can't wait to get back to Honolulu and thaw out.

Gotta flee—
Das Vidanya –
Comrade Chris

December 15, 1970

Dearest Parents—

I know that you two are excellent travelers, but I thought you might like to read this epistle that I've made up for the average TWA passenger.

The Ten Passenger Commandments

1. Thou shalt not worry—he that worrieth hath not joyfulness—remember, few flights are ever fateful.
2. Thou shalt not let other passengers vex thee—thou hast paid through the nose to be gladsome.
3. Rememberest thou, when in Rome (or London, Paris or East Moline) thou shalt be willing to do more or less as the natives do.
4. Thou shalt not pinch, bite, kick, heckle, kiss, fondle or otherwise irk thy flight hostess, or she shall render you exceedingly sorrowful.
5. Thou shalt not attempt to open any doors (i.e., exit, cockpit) other than those leading to the purifying areas.
6. Remember, thou art a guest (albeit, paying) on thy chosen airline—blessed is he that behaveth with respect toward his hostess, for he shall be treateth the selfsame way.
7. Thou shall keep thy diverse children everlastingly tethered to their seats.
8. Thou shalt shun extreme intoxication lest thou find thyself unbeloved by thy fellow travelers.
9. Thou shalt honor thy father and thy mother as well as thy flight hostess, for thou art at her mercy.

10. Thou shalt strive to be of good cheer, for a joyful countenance renders unto thee the likelihood of a blessed flight.

Thus endeth my letter.
Love,
Christine

December 15, 1970

Dear Mary—

The house lights go down - the curtain goes up—a man enters and moves to center stage. "This is Jay Embry," the announcer says, "and he is here to answer all your prayers. He is athletic, he is intellectual, and he is artistic. He is good looking and has a sparkling wit, as well as being sensitive and a gentle and caring lover. And, he is an ex-Marine!"

This is to introduce you to the new love of my life. Oh, Mary, I would rather be with him than in any other place in the world. He's perfect. And, I adore him. He's THE ONE!

Romance and adventure beckon! I'm planning to do my "happily ever afters" with this one.

Love, Chris
P. S. My sister Ann just had a baby girl.

Made in the USA
Las Vegas, NV
20 January 2021

16221381R00173